Flans & Wine

FOOD AND COOKERY
in a
Medieval Monastery

by

Brother William of Berneslei

Translated into modern English
by
David Snowden

First published in Great Britain in 2008 by lulu.com

This edition 2015

www.lulu.com

© 2015 The Vale of Evesham Historical Society

All rights reserved. Apart from any fair dealing for the purpose of private study, research, criticism or review, as permitted under the Copyright, Designs and Patents Act 1988, no part of this publication may be reproduced, stored in any retrieval system or transmitted in any form or by any means, electronic, electrical, chemical, mechanical, optical, photocopying, recording or otherwise, without the prior written permission of the copyright owner. Enquiries should be addressed to the publishers.

CONTENTS

INTRODUCTION		7
TRANSLATOR'S NOTES		11
Who was Whom at Evesham Abbey		11
I. MEAT		**13**
1.	EGURDOUCE	13
2.	BOILED MUTTON	13
3.	MOUNCHELET	14
4.	NEAT'S TONGUE	15
5.	BRAWUNE FRYES	15
6.	BEEF OR MUTTON OLIVES	16
7.	BOURBELIER DE SANGLIER	16
8.	CORMARYE	17
9.	FROSE	17
10.	MORTRESS	18
11.	POURCELET FARCI	18
12.	VENYSON Y-BAKE	19
13.	BRUET SARCENES	20
14.	CAMELINE MEAT BRUET	20
II. POULTRY		**22**
15.	CHICKEN IN ORANGE SAUCE	22
16.	HEN IN WINE-STOCK	23
17.	ENDORED CHICKEN	23
18.	GOOSE OR CAPON FARCED	24
19.	SCHYCONYS WITH THE BRUESSE	24
20.	ROASTED DUCK	25
III. FISH & SEAFOOD		**26**
21.	DAUCE EGRE	26
22.	STEW OF SALMON	27
23.	OYSTRES IN CEVEY	27
24.	DRESSED CRAB	28
25.	PYKES BRASEY	28
26.	SEETH OF FRESH SALMON	29
27.	PIKE IN GALENTYNE	29
IV. BREADS & PASTRIES		**31**
28.	MANCHET	31
29.	HOUSEHOLD BREAD	32
30.	CRUSTE ROLLE	33
31.	PAEST ROYALL	33
V. FLANS & TARTS		**34**
32.	TART DE BRY	34

Flans and Wine

33.	FLAMPOYNTES	34
34.	TARTE IN YMBRE DAY	35
35.	LOMBARD CUSTARD	35

VI. CHEESE, DAIRY & EGGS — 37

36.	PAPYNS	37
37.	ARBOLETTYS	38
38.	LONGE FRETOURE	38
39.	BRUET OF EGGES TO POTAGE	39

VII. DESSERTS & SWEETS — 40

40.	SHREWSBURY CAKES	40
41.	APPLE FRITTERS	40
42.	BRYNDONS	41
43.	PAYNE FOUNDOW	42
44.	TOURTELETES IN FRYTOUR	43
45.	FRUMENTY	43
46.	FRITTER FOR LENT	44
47.	POKEROUNCE	44

VIII. SOUPS & POTTAGES — 45

48.	POTAGE FENE BOILES	45
49.	JOWTES OF ALMAUND MYLKE	45
50.	FRENCH POT HERBS	46
51.	CAWDEL OF MUSKELS	47
52.	APPLE MUSE	47

IX. SAUCES — 49

53.	ALMOND MILK	49
54.	CAMELINE SAUCE	49
55.	GALENTYNE	50
56.	SARACEN SAUCE	50
57.	STOCK	51
58.	STRAWBERYE	51
59.	SAUCE GAUNCILE	52
60.	POIVRE JAUNET	52
61.	RAPEYE	53
62.	COMPOST	53

X. FRUIT & VEGETABLES — 55

63.	DISH OF ASPARAGUS	55
64.	SPYNOCHES Y-FRYED	55
65.	FRIED BEANS	56
66.	SALAT	56
67.	SLYT SOPPES	57

XI. DRINKS — 58

68.	CLARREY	58
69.	POTUS YPOCRAS	58
70.	CAUDELL	59

APPENDIX I. HERBS & SPICES	**61**
APPENDIX II. SPICE MIXTURES	**64**
POUDRE DOUCE	64
POUDRE FORTE	64
SUGAR	64
APPENDIX III. CONVERSION TABLES	**65**
FURTHER READING	**67**
INDEX OF RECIPES	**69**

Flans and Wine

INTRODUCTION

My name is William of Berneslei and I was a monk at the Abbey of St Mary and St Egwin (you probably know it best as Evesham Abbey) in the fifteenth century.

In the sixth century of our Lord, around AD530, the founder of our order, St Benedict (that's him, with his monks, on the front cover) laid down a set of strict rules to be followed by those of us who took the cowl and found our vocation in the cloister. Our food and mealtimes were to be strictly controlled, following the moral framework outlined in *The Rule*, although *The Rule* itself said that certain concessions could be made at the discretion of the abbot.

Our founder said that those who were fitted to take holy orders should be "not given to drinking [and] not a heavy eater". He did not think it seemly that monks should be drunkards or gluttons and this was especially important in a monk who was appointed as a monastery's cellarer.

The Rule said that we should eat two meals each day, dinner (all year round) and supper (Easter to September 14th only). All meals had to be taken during daylight hours so the exact times depended on the season and on the weather. Timing of Vespers, our evening service, also changed so that the service could be completed, and supper eaten, before nightfall.

Some days were fast days. For example on Wednesdays and Fridays between Pentecost and 14th September we were to have no midday meal, unless the abbot decreed otherwise.

The Rule said that we were to refrain entirely from eating the flesh of four-legged beasts, except for monks who were ill and very weak, who may eat flesh: "the eating of meat should be allowed to the sick who are in a weak condition, but when they are restored to health again, all should abstain from meat as usual". "Flesh" was muscle meat, what you would call joints.

The Rule regarding food could also be relaxed for old men and children: "their weaknesses should at all times be taken into consideration, and the letter of *The Rule* should by no means be applied to them in matters of food. Indeed they should always be thought of compassionately, and they should have their meals before the prescribed times". St Benedict also decreed that young boys should receive less food than their elders!

Chapter XXXIX of *The Rule* told us how much food should be prepared. It said that for the daily meal, two dishes should be prepared "to allow for the weaknesses [you would say "the tastes"] of different eaters; so that if someone cannot eat of the one dish he may make a meal of the other". The Rule also allowed for a third dish to be added: "if fruit or tender vegetables are to be had" although we held that vegetables were not food; vegetables were what food ate. Meals were served in "messes", a quantity large enough to provide four or eight portions.

Each Brother was allowed a daily allowance of one pound of bread. The times at which we could eat this were also controlled. On days when there were two meals a third of each monk's bread was held back by the cellarer to accompany supper.

The precise quantities of food could be adjusted at the abbot's bidding if a monk's "work [was] rather heavy". However, St Benedict was adamant that "there must be no danger of over-eating, so that no monk is overtaken by indigestion, for there is nothing so opposed to Christian life as over-eating".

Likewise with drinking. *The Rule* allowed each Brother half a pint of wine a day, at least on special days, but said that "those ... to whom God grants the capacity to abstain should know that they will have their own reward". Greater quantities were permitted if the work was hard or in the heat of summer, but, as our founder said, an abbot "must take care that neither excess nor drunkenness overtakes them. For although we read that wine is not at all a drink for monks, yet, since in our days it is impossible to persuade monks of this, let us agree at least about this that we should not drink our fill, but more sparingly".

Do not judge us too harshly, gentle reader. Alcohol was safer to drink than water in my time and ale especially was drunk in large quantities, both inside and outside the cloister. We were allowed eight pints a day, although this was less on days when wine was issued. I may be forgiven a little pride if I say that our monastic houses were responsible for many improvements in brewing beer. Ale was drunk more in our houses in Northern Europe, where, unlike the home of our founder in Italy, the climate was not so well suited to vineyards. We did have vineyards in Evesham but most of our wine came to us as costly imports. We brewed our own ales at home.

The Rule stressed the importance of living a simple life, so that we would experience a relative poverty, although we never went as hungry as the poor outside our walls. In truth we never went hungry at all. We brethren came from well to do families - I was the second son of a knight of the county - and we ate the sort of food enjoyed by the nobility, the gentry and the élite of the county.

Sadly, some laxity crept into the interpretation of *The Rule* over time, especially in England and those other places far removed from the centre of our Order. It was hard for some of us to comply for we were not peasants to live the peasant life. Our Brothers were reluctant to give up entirely the life to which they were accustomed, regardless of the induced poverty intended in *The Rule*, and indeed St. Benedict had constant criticism of monks that grumbled about their condition: "we lay special stress on this that the brethren remain free from grumbling".

With our centre of authority being so far away, perhaps we had greater opportunity for a more generous interpretation of *The Rule*. However, the Mother Houses were by no means oblivious to the behaviour and excesses of the monks in their lesser houses, and visitations were made periodically, to examine the conduct of the houses of each rule.

Once again I must beg you not to judge us too harshly. *The Rule* was written at Monte Cassino in Italy, where the weather is mild, very different from the harsh weather of England (especially in my day). The Benedictine *Rule*, especially the lack of a second meal from mid-September to the end of Lent (28 to 32 weeks later) may have been easier to sustain in the Mediterranean world. With the exception of our warming-rooms our English monasteries were very cold in winter, and we needed a lot of extra food to keep warm.

I must confess that, when we were given a concession for a particular occasion, we tended to maintain that privilege, even when the occasion had passed. For example we often enjoyed our winter food in summer, too. Many cunning ways were found to interpret *The Rule* so that we could eat irregular foods without, strictly speaking, breaking *The Rule*.

I mentioned that we were not permitted to eat the flesh of four-legged beasts in the refectory, so we had another room, the *misericord*, in which we ate every other day and where flesh meat - and other unusual dishes - could be eaten, while the monks eating in the refectory ate the foods prescribed in *The Rule* (which might include offal as this was not strictly flesh meat). There was also debate over what constituted meat. Was poultry meat in the meaning of *The Rule*? Birds have only two legs! In fact St. Thomas Aquinas, at one point, stipulated that chickens were aquatic in origin; therefore, because they counted as fish, they could be eaten on fast days. At richer monasteries, such as ours, rabbits were bred for their embryos (please do not shudder, they are delicious fried) because these did not count as meat either.

As well as our usual food we often received "pittances". A pittance was a special dish, often of the richest food, eaten on feast days of Saints, as well as on other important occasions such as the anniversary of our founder. It was astounding how many saints we venerated in those days! So many so that we needed a Pittancer to work alongside the Kitchener and prepare these special dishes.

How much did we eat? We had no way to count our food except by weight, whereas you count your food in calories so I will put it in your terms: on average we used to have around 7,000 calories a day, all found.

Many were the chances to over-eat and your physicians would not think our diet healthy: low in fresh fruit and vegetables, while high in fat. Perhaps this is why many of us, even when quite young, suffered the torment of arthritis of the knee, the hip and the hand.

But enough gloom! In the rest of this book I have set out some recipes that were popular at Evesham Abbey. If you read through our papers, and particularly look at the accounts of the Kitchener and Cellarer, you will find many more. I have tried to choose dishes where the ingredients are available in your time and I have written down quantities, and cooking times and temperatures, so that you will be able to use them. There is also a chapter on what to drink, including some favourite hot drinks that we concocted on cold days.

Why did I call this book: "Flans and Wine"? Because, as a special treat on feast days, that is what we were given. I hope that you find this little book a treat, also ...

- **WILLIAM OF BERNESLEI**

Flans and Wine

Translator's Notes

It is not my intention to present a dissertation on the eating habits of fifteenth century monks as there are several excellent books on the topic. The purpose of this translation of Brother William's manuscripts is simply to make a collection of 70 fifteenth century recipes available to adventurous modern cooks in a style that is easy to read and follow. I hope that I have succeeded in this noble purpose.

There were no published books of recipes in the fifteenth century and the recipes in this book were a personal view. You are free to experiment and to vary them to suit your personal taste. Whatever you do, you cannot be wrong (short of infringing the laws against poisoning)!

I have put nothing in about medieval cooking methods, nor about the utensils or vessels used in the period. That is the province of the medieval re-enactor and living history expert, who will be delighted to discuss them with you, and to demonstrate their use at length. These recipes have been calculated to allow you to produce authentic-tasting dishes without having to obtain a degree in medieval history or to turn your kitchen into a replica of its fifteenth century equivalent.

NOTE: except where stated, the recipes make enough for a "mess" of eight small portions or four larger ones. The recipes call for fresh herbs. If you use dried herbs then halve the quantities. Ground black pepper and sea salt will be most authentic.

Who was Whom at Evesham Abbey

The Cellarer of Evesham Abbey supervised his monks and lay brothers in the production and storage of food and drink. The Kitchener provided staff to work in the kitchen and ensured that it had sufficient fuel for cooking. He also supervised the apple and pear groves (for cider) and the beehives. Good quality sugar was imported from North Africa. It was scarce and expensive and had to be kept locked away when not required. Instead honey was the principal sweetener in most of the dishes. The hives also provided beeswax for candles. The Refectorer organised the serving and clearing of meals and the washing up afterwards. The Almoner distributed (or "doled") alms to the poor of Evesham. He provided doles of various sorts including clothing and, rarely, money but most alms were in the form of food: black bread, ale and leftovers from the refectory's tables. The house where the Almoner worked stood outside the great gatehouse of the abbey and it remains today as the Almonry Heritage Centre and Museum.

- David Snowden

The proceeds from this book of recipes will be donated to help finance the work of the Almonry Heritage Centre and Museum, Evesham.

Flans and Wine

I. Meat

Meat was the food of the nobility, which is why the name of the beasts differed from their meat when served up in portions. The meat from a cow (eng.) was beef (fr. boeffe), from a pig (eng.) was pork (fr. porc) and from a sheep (eng.) was mutton (fr. mouton). However, meat was forbidden to us for much of the year. The church dictated abstinence from meat and all other animal products every Wednesday, Friday and Saturday, on the eve of festivals and during the 40 days of Lent. On the days when we could eat meat we fared very well, as you will see …

1. Egurdouce

"Egurdouce" means "sour and sweet" and you can also cook it as all "sweet" (leave out the vinegar) or all "sour" (leave out the sugar). But for the authentic taste try this recipe. The meat we used was kid or rabbit; lamb is an acceptable substitute for kid. The sauce of the dish can be as thick as you like, adding breadcrumbs to thicken it. You can add chopped parsley, sage and other leafy herbs to taste.

2-3lb of stewing lamb cut into chunks or 1 rabbit jointed and cut up
2 tablespoons of butter
¼ cup of currants
2-3 white onions
1½ cups of red wine
½ cup of wine or cider vinegar
½ cup of sugar
½ teaspoon each of ginger and cinnamon
¼ teaspoon of pepper
1 teaspoon of salt, to taste
2 tablespoons of breadcrumbs

Melt the butter in a frying pan and brown the meat in it. When it is almost brown enough add the currants. Meanwhile cover the onions with cold water and bring them to the boil. Drain off the water and chop the onions. Add the onions to the meat and currants and fry for a few more minutes. Add the wine, vinegar, sugar and seasonings. Cover the pan and simmer for around 45 minutes. Mix the breadcrumbs with some of the sauce to form a paste and stir it in until the sauce is as thick as you require.

2. Boiled Mutton

The Cotswolds were sheep country and the abbey owned several thousand head of sheep so mutton was a readily available meat. In this recipe the cook uses cold roast lamb (we had

Flans and Wine

mutton, as you may, but you will probably enjoy it more with tender lamb). If you prefer a slightly sweeter dish then add sugar or honey to taste.

1lb of cold roast lamb
2 teaspoons of finely chopped parsley
1 medium white onion, finely chopped
2inch stick of cinnamon
Salt and pepper to taste
A pinch of saffron (or a few drops of yellow food colouring)
2 teaspoons of red wine vinegar
7 fl oz of red wine

Chop the meat into small pieces and put it into a saucepan. Add the parsley, onion and cinnamon and season it well. Sprinkle the saffron or food colouring over the meat then add the vinegar and wine. Bring the mixture to the boil and cook it until the onion is soft and transparent and the meat is heated through. If it looks too dry add a little extra wine, but do not make it too runny. When the liquid is almost the consistency of a syrup it is ready to serve.

3. Mounchelet

This dish resembles your blanquette de veau and, although it can be made with several types of white meat (particularly lamb or pork) veal is definitely the preferable meat for the dish.

1½-2lb stewing veal
2 medium white onions
1 tablespoon of finely chopped parsley
1 teaspoon each of thyme, rosemary and savoury
¼ teaspoon of each of ground ginger and coriander
1½-2 cups of chicken stock
1 cup of white wine
1 egg
1 tablespoon of white wine or cider vinegar
Salt to taste

Cut the veal into small squares and put them into a large saucepan. Add the onions, herbs and spices and cover them with the wine and stock. Bring to the boil, reduce the heat, cover and simmer for 45 minutes. Beat the egg with the vinegar and pour a little of the hot sauce into this mixture, stirring all the time. Make sure that the sauce is hot but NOT boiling. Take the saucepan off the heat and add the mixture to its contents. Stir the mixture over a very low heat to thicken, taking care that the mixture does not boil after the egg has been added.

4. Neat's Tongue

In my day we prepared salted ox tongues in water, finely chopped them and mixed them with herbs and spices to provide a warming dish for a winter's day.

1 ox tongue
1 tablespoon of chopped parsley
1 teaspoon of chopped mint
2 teaspoons of chopped sage
Salt and pepper, to taste
1 tablespoon of olive oil
Wine or cider vinegar

Boil the ox tongue in salted water until it is done, remove it from the water and drain well. Mince the tongue or chop it very finely. Mix the meat with the freshly chopped herbs. Heat the olive oil in a deep frying pan and gently sauté the meat and herb mixture until the meat has warmed and the herbs have become aromatic. Add the salt and pepper to taste. Put the meat in a serving dish and pour a little vinegar over the top just before serving.

5. Brawune Fryes

These pork fritters were a great favourite, probably because of the sugar in the recipe. You will probably have gathered from other recipes in this little book that we liked to mix sweet with savoury, particularly when cooking pork.

¼ cup of plain flour
2 eggs, well beaten
2 tablespoons of sugar (plus one teaspoon for the topping)
Pinch of saffron (or a drop of yellow food colouring)
1 teaspoon of salt
1½lb of raw pork (preferably fillet) cut into ¼ inch strips
4 tablespoons of lard

First make the batter by mixing the flour, eggs, 2 tablespoons of sugar, saffron (or food colouring) and salt. Mix the batter well and then add the strips of pork, making sure to coat each one thoroughly. Heat the lard in a large frying pan (if you object to lard use olive oil instead) over a medium heat. Carefully place the strips of pork into the frying pan so that each is separate from the others and no two are touching. Fry the meat, turning once, until the batter is brown on both sides and the pork is cooked (test with a skewer). This should take between 5 and 10 minutes. Remove the meat from the pan and drain it to remove the fat or oil. Arrange the strips of meat on a dish or plate and sprinkle with 1 teaspoon of sugar.

6. Beef or Mutton Olives

This simple dish provides a tasty treat for meat days.

4 thin slices of topside of beef or rump of lamb
1 large white onion
6 hard-boiled egg yolks
1 tablespoon of shredded suet
2 teaspoons of parsley, finely chopped
Pinch of ground ginger
Pinch of powdered saffron (or a drop of yellow food colouring)
Salt
Butter
Cider vinegar
Poudre douce (see page 64).

Beat the slices of meat thin with a steak tenderiser or rolling pin. Finely chop the onion and egg yolks together and add the suet, parsley, ginger, saffron (or food colouring) and salt to taste. Knead the stuffing mixture into a paste, using the juice of the onion to bind. If there is insufficient juice use a little extra water. Spread the stuffing on the meat slices and roll them up, securing each roll with a small wooden skewer. Grease a baking tin and lay the rolls side by side in the tin with the open edges underneath. Speckle the rolls with butter and bake them in an oven at 350°F for 35-40 minutes. Baste once or twice while the olives are baking. Lay the cooked olives on a serving dish and sprinkle with cider vinegar, poudre douce and the remaining egg yolks, crumbled.

7. Bourbelier de Sanglier

I hear that wild boar once again are running free in England so it should be possible to obtain their meat in the shops. If, however, it is not on the meat counter at your local supermarket you can use a loin of pork (as our cooks often did). To give your pork more of a period taste you might marinade the pork for three or four days in a mixture of red wine, wine or cider vinegar, olive oil and any selection of dried herbs that you favour.

4-6lb loin of boar or pork
Whole cloves
½ teaspoon of each of ground ginger, cardamom, pepper and salt
¼ teaspoon of each of cinnamon, ground cloves and nutmeg
¼ cup of red wine
1 cup of wine or cider vinegar
2 tablespoons of breadcrumbs

Put the loin of boar or pork into a roasting pan and stud it with the whole cloves at 1 inch intervals. Mix the other ingredients thoroughly and pour the mixture over the joint. Roast as usual (see your oven's instruction book for times and temperatures), basting occasionally. When the meat is roasted pour off the juices from the roasting pan into a saucepan. Skim off the grease and bring the pan to the boil, stirring in the breadcrumbs to thicken the sauce. When you have the sauce at the consistency you require you may either pour the sauce over the meat or serve it separately.

8. Cormarye

This recipe is a little more labour intensive than most of those in this little book. It involves preparing a marinade, marinading the meat, using the marinade to baste the meat and then using the marinade and dripping to form a sauce.

5-7lb loin of pork
1-2 teaspoons each of coriander and caraway seed
2-3 cloves of garlic, crushed
1 cup of red wine
½ teaspoon of salt
¼ teaspoon of ground black pepper

You will need to grind the coriander and caraway seeds carefully, using a mortar and pestle or a grinder. A blender may not do a thorough job. When you have ground the seeds as finely as you can, add the remaining ingredients for the sauce and blend them thoroughly. You will need a pan or other container into which the pork will only just fit, leaving little space all round. Prick the pork, put it in the container and pour the sauce mixture over it. Leave it to marinade for at least two hours, preferably four. Put everything into a roasting pan and roast it in the usual way (see your oven's instruction book for times and temperatures) basting occasionally with the juices from the pan. When the meat is roasted pour off the juices from the roasting pan into a saucepan. Skim off the grease and bring the pan to the boil. For a thicker sauce stir in breadcrumbs as in ***recipe 7***. When you have the sauce at the consistency you require you may either pour the sauce over the meat or serve it separately.

9. Frose

A popular way of cooking fish or white meat was to combine it with eggs. On a meat day we would eat pork cooked that way. On a fish day we used trout or mullet, or some other sweet-water fish. Trout and mullet are available from your supermarkets. For a meat day take 1lb of bacon, ham or pork cut into stewing-sized pieces. For a fish day take 1lb of fresh fish fillets, cut into pieces. You will also need …

Olive oil
6 eggs, well beaten
2 tablespoons of cooking fat (dripping or lard) or butter
Salt and pepper

Cut the meat or fish into pieces and fry in a little olive oil until just done. Do not over-cook it. Remove it from the pan and drain it. Chop the meat or fish into small pieces then mix

Flans and Wine

into the beaten eggs. Melt the fat or butter in a large pan (if you are cooking fish use butter) heat and, when hot, add the mixture of meat and eggs. Season with a little salt and pepper and cook on a medium heat. As the egg begins to thicken stir it with a wooden spoon as if you were scrambling eggs and continue until the mixture has completely thickened then serve immediately.

10. Mortress

This was a versatile dish that could be served thin, as a sort of soup, or thick, as a meat paste. We ate it thick as a paste or paté, which is what this recipe will produce if you follow it closely.

1 cup of cooked chicken, minced
1 cup of cooked pork, minced
¼ cup of cooked pork and chicken livers, minced
4 cups of stock (without breadcrumbs)
½ to 1 cup of unseasoned breadcrumbs
3 egg yolks
1 teaspoon of pepper
1 teaspoon of cloves
1 teaspoon of ginger
1 tablespoon of sugar
A pinch of saffron (in the absence of saffron a drop of yellow food colouring will suffice)
Salt to taste
A mixture of 1 tablespoon of ginger and 1 tablespoon of sugar as a garnish.

Bring the stock to the boil, add the minced chicken, pork and livers and bring back to the boil. Reduce the heat and stir in the breadcrumbs, egg yolks and all of the spices. Allow the mixture to cook for several minutes. If it is too thin add more breadcrumbs. If you would prefer it thinner add more stock. Serve garnished with the mixture of ginger and sugar.

11. Pourcelet Farci

I have included this as it is one of our grander dishes, the sort of thing people in your day think we ate all of the time. In reality it was an elaborate banqueting dish that we occasionally enjoyed in the misericord and that you might want to provide for an unusual party dish or family celebration – this recipe serves 10 – or you could scale it down using a joint of pork.

1 20-25lb sucking pig or piglet
8lb pork roast (without bone or fat)
1½lb pig's liver
2 dozen hard-boiled egg yolks, chopped
2lb brie

1 lb peeled roasted chestnuts
2 tablespoon each of salt & pepper (to taste)
1 tablespoons each of ginger, cloves, & sugar (to taste)
2 cups olive oil
2 cups red wine vinegar
½ teaspoon of salt
Butcher's needle and thread

Chop the pork roast into small pieces and grill or boil it until well done. If you boil it add a little salt and pepper to the water and save the stock for later. After the pork has cooled, mince or dice the meat very small and set it aside. Cut the liver into small pieces, grill or boil until well done and then drain and cool. Mince or dice the cooled liver very small and set it aside. Mince or grind the flesh of the chestnuts and chop the brie as small as possible. Mix the roast pork, pig's liver, chopped egg yolks, brie, chestnuts and spices and mix thoroughly with your hands. For a smoother stuffing, add enough of the reserved stock to thoroughly moisten the mixture. Adjust the spices to taste. Stuff the pig or joint with the meat mixture and sew the opening shut when you have finished. Place the stuffed pig or joint on parchment paper on a large baking sheet or tray. If using a whole piglet cover the ears, the snout and the tail with aluminium foil to prevent over-cooking. Pre-heat your oven to 400°F.

Mix the oil, vinegar and salt in a small saucepan and bring it to a slow simmer. Baste the pig thoroughly before placing it in the oven. Cook the stuffed pig for three to four hours, basting thoroughly every 15 minutes, until it has completely cooked through. (You can use a meat thermometer to check that the centre of the roast is over 175°F. We had to guess).

When the pig is completely roasted, remove it from the oven. Remove the aluminium foil from the ears, snout and tail and carefully transfer the pig to a large cutting board or garnished serving tray. Make a special presentation of the whole pig to your lucky guests, then carve and serve. You might like to provide dishes of *Poivre Jaunet* or *Cameline Sauce*.

12. Venyson Y-bake

Meat pies of various types were very popular in my day and in this one we cooked venison (usually supplied to our abbot as a gift) with honey and egg yolks, which make the pie much less dry then the plain venison pie that we also enjoyed. If you want to cheat you can buy a ready made pie shell or, to be authentic, you can use the pastry recipe on page 33 (***recipe 31***).

1½ lb of venison, parboiled and minced or chopped small
⅓ cup of honey
4 egg yolks
½ tsp of salt
½ tsp each of pepper and ginger
9" pie shell with lid

Mix the ingredients, place them in the pie shell and add the lid. Bake at 375°F fof 45-50 minutes or until the crust is golden brown.

13. Bruet Sarcenes

In medieval Europe we thought of Saracens (you would call them "Arabs") as having skin of a deep brown-red shade and this dish is coloured in imitation. To provide the colour we used alkanet, a red dye made from the roots of the alkanet plant. You can use red food colouring as long as you make sure that the final colour is a deep, rich red. This is another dish that works well with venison. However, when venison was not available, we used beef or pork. For a richer dish add raisins, currants, pine nuts and almonds to the sauce, to taste.

2lb of venison, beef or pork
2 cups Almond Milk (made with reserved stock; see recipe below)
1 small onion, chopped
8 tbs of rice flour
½ tsp of ground cloves
½ tsp each of cubeb (or milled black pepper) nutmeg and mace
½ cup of red wine
1 tbs of sugar
Red food colouring (a few drops)
Salt to taste

Cut the meat into pieces, put it in a pot, cover it with water and bring it to the boil. When boiling reduce the heat and simmer until the meat is tender. Drain the meat, reserving the stock. Allow the meat to cool and then cube it into bite-sized pieces. Set the meat aside. Make the Almond Milk (see recipe 53 on page 49) but using two cups of the reserved stock instead of water. Sauté the onion until it is just tender then drain it and it add to the almond milk and blend in the flour until the mixture is thick and smooth. Add the cloves. Slowly bring the Almond Milk to the boil, stirring occasionally to prevent it sticking. Reduce the heat, add the additional spices, wine and food colouring and allow it to cook for several more minutes. If the sauce becomes too thick add more wine or stock. Remove the sauce from the heat and toss the meat with enough of the sauce to thoroughly coat the pieces of meat but no more. Serve it at once on platters or in bowls. You can eat the bite-sized pieces, coated in sauce, with your fingers (as we did) or you can use a fork if you must.

14. Cameline Meat Bruet

This is a cold dish of thin slices of beef pickled in Cameline Sauce. Most bruets or "brewets" were cooked but some were not, as this, which makes enough for four to eight portions.

2lb beef, sliced into thin strips
1 tsp of butter or olive oil
1 tsp of salt
⅛ tsp of pepper
Cameline Sauce (see recipe 54 on page 49)

Melt the butter or heat the olive oil in a pan. Add the meat and the seasonings and sauté until done. Drain well and set aside to cool. Put the meat in a container with a tight fitting lid and add enough Cameline Sauce to cover the meat. Put the top on and refrigerate for several days, taking the container out and shaking it once a day. To eat, remove the meat from the marinade and serve it at room temperature.

II. POULTRY

The church officially forbade us to eat the meat of "four-legged" animals in the refectory but there were no such restrictions on "two-legged" meat so we made great use of poultry, wildfowl, game birds and waterfowl. The abbey employed its own bird catcher, we bargained with local poulterers for supplies and we kept our own stock cooped and fattened on the barton, the abbey's own farm land. We practiced battery farming of poultry in the fifteenth century. However, eggs were precious so we tended to eat birds that were bought or caught before we consumed our own. The variety of birds eaten in the abbey was much greater than you would eat in your day. Crane, heron, gull, quail, curlew, egret, plover, snipe, thrush, bittern, greenfinch, blackbird and lapwing were all served as dishes at our meals. However, in selecting these recipes I have chosen birds that you will easily find in your shops.

15. Chicken in Orange Sauce

In your day you take such luxuries as oranges for granted but, in the fifteenth century, they were one of those costly foodstuffs that had to be imported into England. Our cook used bitter oranges, what you would call "Seville" oranges. You may have difficulty finding suitable oranges and ordinary eating oranges will give a different flavour. However, there is an equivalent easy to make by blending six parts of orange juice with two parts of grapefruit juice and one part of lime juice. This tastes like bitter orange. This recipe uses verjuice, a common ingredient in medieval cookery. It is the juice of sour unripe grapes and some wineries produce it. Sour grape juice can also be bought from middle eastern grocers. If you cannot find this you can make a serviceable substitute by mixing equal parts of lemon juice and dryish white wine.

2-3 small chickens, partridges or pigeons
3 bitter oranges or 3 sweet oranges, 3 tablespoons of grapefruit juice and 1 tablespoon of lime juice (all fresh, of course)
¼ cup of verjuice or half-and-half lemon juice and white wine

You can either spit-roast the birds (or buy them ready roasted, dare I say?) or you may follow the instructions that came with your oven and simply roast the birds. Make the sauce when the birds are nearly done. Cut each orange into four slices with the skin left on. Put them into a large saucepan with the other ingredients including the bitter orange juice substitute, if necessary. Bring the sauce to a boil then reduce the heat and simmer it for 15 minutes to reduce the liquid a little while softening the orange peels. Test the sauce and add sugar if necessary. It should be bitter but not too bitter. Cut the birds into serving-size portions, put them into the saucepan with the sauce and simmer them for another 15 minutes, basting the meat with the sauce and turning the pieces occasionally so that they cook thoroughly in the sauce. Serve with good crusty bread to sop up the juices.

16. Hen in Wine-Stock

The use of extra stock, thickened with bread crumbs and flavoured with vinegar, is a necessary aspect of this dish's preparation, and was commonly used in other dishes. The breadcrumb, stock and vinegar mixture not only thickens the sauce but makes an excellent binding agent for the cinnamon, which does not need to be strained out as is specified in many other of our sauces containing the spice we called "canella". We called a stock of wine "dubatte", which was a corruption of the French "jus batard" ("batard" is "bastard", a sweet Spanish wine). This recipe will feed four to six people.

1 chicken, roasted and in pieces
3 cups chicken stock
2 cups verjuice, sour grape juice or mild red wine
½ teaspoon each of cloves, mace, pepper and cinnamon
¼ cup of bread crumbs
½ teaspoon of vinegar

Bring two cups of the stock, the juice/wine and the spices to a boil then reduce the heat to a simmer. In a separate saucepan bring the remaining stock to the boil. Add the breadcrumbs and vinegar, stirring well until the mixture is thick and smooth. Remove if from the heat and add it to the mixture of stock and juice/wine, stirring constantly until it is well blended into a gravy-like sauce (or you could cheat and put the whole mixture through a food processor or blender). Put the chicken pieces into a large pan, pour the mixture over the pieces and bring it to the boil. Reduce the heat and simmer it for several minutes until the sauce and the chicken are thoroughly cooked together.

17. Endored Chicken

Our cook prepared this dish with whole chickens with just the breast bones removed. If you are not a skilled chef or carver, and you know no-one who will help, you may find it difficult to obtain a bird ready to roast. Your local butcher might be able to help you. Otherwise you could do what our cook did, scalding the chicken first, then pulling out the breast bone while leaving the skin intact and all of the other bones in place. If you are not feeling so adventurous, then do not despair. Endoring in this manner was common in our kitchens and any cut or portion of the chicken, with or without bones, will do. But please remember to leave the skin on.

1 chicken, whole or in pieces, and boneless if possible
Egg yolks, beaten, as required

Roast the chicken until done (look at the instructions that come with your oven for the exact time). Remove from the oven, brush with egg yolk, and return briefly to the oven until the glaze is set, which should take about one minute. Be careful not to overcook the chicken; the trick is to make the chicken yellow, not brown. Repeat the glaze a few times if you want a brighter shade of yellow.

18. Goose or Capon Farced

In this recipe I have bowed to modern tastes and have suggested that you should sauté the onion and parsley and then mix them with the other ingredients to make the stuffing. Originally we parboiled all the ingredients together. However, David (my translator) tells me that the boiled version may not be to everyone's taste. But do not let that stop you trying it if you wish to be adventurous. The recipe calls for onions and grapes. If you do not like onions use only the grapes, and vice versa. Either will still provide an authentic taste. By the way, in case you do not know, a capon is a castrated male bird.

1 goose or capon
24 hard-boiled egg yolks, chopped
2lb of seedless grapes (white or red)
4 bunches of fresh parsley, chopped
3-4 large white onions, chopped
1 tablespoon each of ginger, pepper, cinnamon and salt
¼lb of butter

Sauté the onions and parsley together in the butter until the onion softens. Mix the grapes, egg yolks and spices, add the butter, onions and parsley and mix well. Stuff the goose or capon with this mixture and put it in a roasting pan. Rub a little oil (olive oil is good) into the skin, sprinkle it with salt and pepper and then roast it at 400° F for 2-3 hours for the goose or for 1-2 hours for the capon, until the bird is tender and has turned a deep golden brown.

19. Schyconys with the Bruesse

Brewes (or "bruesse") were pieces of stale bread or toast used in dishes that would otherwise be too liquid (do you call these "croutons"?). Cooking chicken with beef may seem like an unusual combination but it was one of our favourites.

1 chicken cut into pieces
2lb stewing beef, cut into large pieces
1 tablespoon each of parsley, sage and savoury
1 teaspoon of salt
Pinch of saffron (or a few drops of yellow food colouring)
4 pieces of toasted bread, cut into thin strips

Put the chicken and beef into a large pan and cover them with water. Bring them to the boil. Reduce the heat to a simmer then stir in the spices. Allow the dish to cook slowly until the chicken and beef are tender. Place the strips of toasted bread on a serving dish, pour a little of the stock over the bread and then place the chicken pieces on top and spoon the rest of the mixture over them.

20. Roasted Mallard

To medieval monks ducks counted as fish because they originated in the water, which made duck dishes very popular because we could eat them on "fish" days! We favoured mallard and our cook created rich sauces to serve with it. This recipe combines honey, mustard and ale ("real" ale).

1 duck, 6-8lb (it need not be a mallard!)
3-4 large white onions, minced or chopped very small
Duck fat (or you could use olive oil)
1 large white onion, minced or chopped very small (another one)
2 cups of "real" ale
½ cup of Dijon mustard
½ cup of clear honey

Stuff the duck with the 3-4 chopped onions and bake or roast it until it is done (see the instructions for your oven for the time). Remove some of the fat from the roasting tin and put it in a frying pan with the extra chopped onion. Fry the onion until it is translucent then lower the heat to a simmer and slowly blend in the ale, mustard and honey until you have a smooth and slightly thick sauce. Simmer it gently for a few minutes and then serve it with the roasted duck.

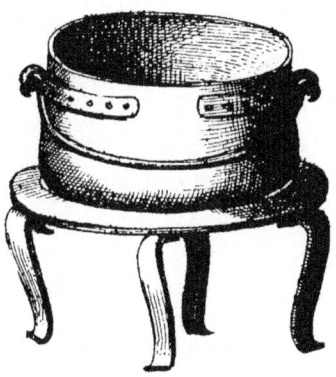

III. FISH & SEAFOOD

Fish was a major part of our diet. The Church laid down that Fridays were fish days, as were Saturdays and Wednesdays. No one may eat meat on those days and throughout Lent eggs and other dairy foods were forbidden too, so that for half of the year our diet was (officially) fish.

For ordinary people "fish" meant salted or pickled herrings. England's herring fleets brought in great quantities during the summer and they were salted and pickled for transport inland. "Stockfish", another staple, was dried cod and hard as a board; herring and stockfish fed most of the inland population. Our brethren at Westminster, and others near the coast, were able to eat oysters, whelks and winkles.

We enjoyed plentiful river fish such as salmon, trout, grayling, bream and tench, as well as eels from the Avon. We also had our own fishponds, called "stews", in which we bred carp (a rare treat) and pike (a common dish). Pickled salmon was a luxury imported from Scotland and Ireland when out of season in England.

On occasion we were able to enjoy sea fish including most of those that you eat: plaice, haddock and mackerel, as well as more exotic breeds. Seals were food as were the "royal" fish: whale, sturgeon and porpoise. These belonged to the king but he occasionally made a present to our abbot. Crab and lobster were also popular.

We ate some strange creatures as "fish". Barnacle geese and puffins counted as fish because they were said to be created at sea. Beavers (there were still beavers in our rivers in my day) were fish because they had fishes' tails.

Salt fish soon became unappetising so many spices and herb sauces were prepared with them. Parsley, a common garnish for fish was fried before being sprinkled on the dish.

21. Dauce Egre

Here is fish in a sweet and sour sauce. The fish must be fresh and either whole (apart from being cleaned and gutted) in fillets or cut into steaks. Haddock is ideal for this recipe.

Enough fresh fish to serve 2-3 people
Olive oil
2 cups of red wine vinegar
¹/₃ of a cup of sugar
1 medium sized white onion, finely chopped or grated
½ teaspoon each of mace and cloves
1 teaspoon of ground cubeb (if you cannot find cubeb use black pepper)

Poach the fish until it is just done then remove it from the water and drain it well. Put the red wine vinegar, sugar, onions and spices into a saucepan. Taste and adjust the sweet (sugar) and sour (vinegar) until you have a pleasing balance. Bring the sauce to the boil then reduce the heat and continue cooking until the onions are soft and transparent. Heat a little olive oil in a frying pan and fry the fish on both sides until they have turned a crispy light brown. Remove the fish from the oil and drain it. Put the fish on a platter or individual plates and pour the sauce over it.

22. Stew of Salmon

Another Lenten dish, a mildly flavoured stew of salmon in which the smoothness of the salmon contrasts with crunchy pine nuts and blanched almonds. The recipe calls for the use of galingale, an asian root similar to ginger. You might find it in ethnic groceries, dried and ready ground. Otherwise you may have to grind it yourself. Galingale is a tough fibrous spice and will gum up or even break an electric grinder so you may have to resort to the ancient mortar and pestle or the modern hammer! If you cannot find galingale use a mixture of equal parts of ginger and pepper.

2lb of salmon fillet
¼ cup of verjuice or equal parts of lemon juice and dry white wine
½ cup of water
½ teaspoon each of ground ginger, ground galingale (or substitute) and ground black pepper
½ cup each of pine nuts, blanched almonds and raisins
1 tablespoon each of chopped marjoram, fresh chopped mint and chopped parsley

Cut the salmon into small chunks and put them into a heavy saucepan that has a lid. Mix the spices, water and verjuice (or substitute) and pour it over the salmon. Simmer until the salmon is half cooked then add the remaining ingredients and cook until the salmon is done.

23. Oystres in Cevey

Oysters may be a rich man's food in your day but back in the fifteenth century they were everyday fare, even for the common man. This is a recipe for stewed oysters that might have been found on our refectory table or in a well-off man's hall.

1 dozen shelled oysters (keep the juice)
1 cup of white wine
2 tablespoons of butter
2 small onions, finely chopped
3 tablespoons of breadcrumbs
½ teaspoon of cinnamon
Salt and pepper
Pinch of saffron (or a few drops of yellow food colouring)
1 tablespoon of red wine vinegar

Flans and Wine

Melt the butter in a frying pan and fry the chopped onions until they are soft. Put them aside. Put the oysters, oyster juice and wine into a large saucepan and bring it to the boil. Reduce the heat and simmer for 4 to 5 minutes or until the edges of the oysters curl. Remove the pan from the heat, cover it and let it sit for 20 minutes. Chop the oysters and set them aside. Put the wine stock in its saucepan onto a medium heat, add the breadcrumbs, onions, vinegar (to taste) and the spices. Bring to the boil and reduce the stock until it has thickened, stirring all the time. Remove it from the heat, add the oysters and serve hot.

24. Dressed Crab

Crabs were a rare treat, brought alive either overland or up the river Avon in barrels of brine. A cook had to know how to dress a crab and this is a simple but enjoyable recipe.

2 cups of crab meat, cooked and shredded (if you are using fresh crab be sure to save the shell)
¼ cup of cider vinegar
¼-½ cup of red wine
1 teaspoon each of ginger and cinnamon
1 tablespoon of sugar or to taste
1 whole crab shell or ramekin
1 pinch of sugar & cinnamon

Combine the crab meat, cider vinegar, ginger, cinnamon and sugar and blend them thoroughly with a fork (or you might try the modern equivalent of passing food through a strainer – the food processor). The mixture should have the consistency of a pâté. Use more or less wine as necessary. Fill the crab shell or ramekin with the crabmeat and brown it in an oven at 425°F oven or under a moderate grill. Sprinkle a little cinnamon and sugar on top and serve hot.

25. Pykes Brasey

Pike are freshwater game fish, similar to carp. You may be able to buy fresh carp or pike, from a specialist fishmonger but, if you cannot, your local supermarket should be able to sell you a whole fish from their seafood or frozen food sections. You will need fish that have been gutted and cleaned (an unappealing task that you may not wish to do at home) but left whole. If all else fails, use any cut of fresh fish that you can obtain.

2- 4 small to medium-sized fish, gutted and cleaned
2 cups of red or white wine
1½ teaspoons of ginger
1 tablespoon of sugar, or to taste
Salt to taste

Roast or grill the fish until it is cooked through. Bring the wine to the boil, reduce the heat and then add the spices and sugar, stirring until the sugar is dissolved. Lay the cooked fish on a serving dish and cover it with the wine sauce, or present the sauce as an accompaniment in a separate serving dish.

26. Seeth of Fresh Salmon

There are numerous ways to cook salmon. In this one the fish is poached ("seethed") in water, ale, salt and herbs.

4 Salmon steaks (or any variety of fish)
1 cup water
1 cup beer or ale
¼ cup white wine vinegar
¼ teaspoon of salt
3 tablespoons of parsley flakes
1 teaspoon of thyme
1 teaspoon of rosemary leaves

Leaving the fish on one side combine all of the ingredients in a saucepan, bring to a boil, reduce the heat and simmer. Put the fish in a shallow baking dish then add enough of the beer mixture to cover the fish to two thirds of its depth. Cover the baking dish then put it in an oven at 425°F for around 15-20 minutes or until the fish becomes tender and flakes with a fork when pierced. Remove the fish from the baking dish and serve.

27. Pike in Galentyne

This is another recipe for cooking pike (or similar fish) and one much used for meals of fish at the abbey. It uses a version of galentyne (***recipe 55***) slightly modified to make a less rich "house-wife's sauce". If you are using pike be aware that it has a line of thin bones through the middle of the flesh on each side; be sure to remove all of these (see below).

3lb middle cut of pike or similar large fish
1¼ cups of white wine
2 tablespoons of white wine vinegar
2-3 stalks of parsley
Salt
3 slices of brown bread with the crusts removed
¼ teaspoon of ground cinnamon
⅛ teaspoon of ground white pepper
4oz of white onions, peeled and chopped
Olive Oil

Flans and Wine

Put the fish into a deep frying pan, add the white wine, wine vinegar and parsley. Add enough salted water to cover the fish and poach it gently for 15 minutes. Turn off the heat and leave the fish to finish cooking in the cooling liquid, covering the pan and leaving the fish until it is tepid. Lift the fish out of the frying pan, taking care not to break the pieces, and put the pan liquid on one side. Put the bread in a large bowl and add enough of the pan liquid to cover it. Remove the skin from the fish and take out the spine and other bones (see above). Cut the flesh of the fish into small pieces. Strain the pan liquid into a clean pan. Blend the soaked bread, cinnamon, pepper and two cups of the pan liquid either by hand (authentic) or in your blender (sensibly modern). Turn this mixture out into the rest of the pan liquid. Fry the onions in a little oil until soft and transparent and add them to the pan liquid. Season to taste, add the pieces of fish and re-heat them gently to serve.

You can serve this as a cold dish, if you like, when it takes on the complexion of "pike in aspic". Because you are cooking only the middle part of the fish the sauce will not reliably gel by itself (if you cooked the fish whole it *would* gel by itself) so you will need to add a little gelatine. Do it like this ... keep the fried onions and the fish pieces aside while you season the liquid. Reheat the liquid with enough gelatine to firm it up. Add the onions and fish pieces, turn it out into a mould (fish shaped?) and leave it to set in a refrigerator or other cold place.

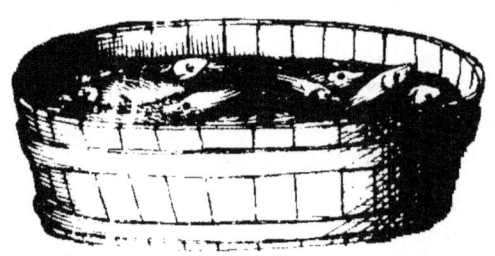

IV. Breads & Pastries

Bread was our staple food, as it was for everyone, but the quality of the bread varied from place to place, the grains available locally and, of course, one's income. The finest whitest bread was made from wheat. Wheat grew on good soil and only a landed estate could give over rich soil and valuable manure for it. Our cook used wheat from the abbey's own estates, ground in our own mill, sifted two or three times and baked into a loaf called "pandemain", of the finest quality. "Wastel" was another top quality white bread (actually more of a yellow bread as our miller did not include chalk or "creta preparata" to bleach the flour). A slightly cheaper white bread was called "cocket".

The most common bread was called "maslin". We made it from a mixture of wheat flour and rye flour. Darker bread was made from rye flour alone. "Cheat" was what you would call "wholemeal bread", baked from wheat with the coarse bran sifted out. We also had "tourte", called "brown bread", which contained husk as well as flour.

By my time at the abbey we could eat from wooden, or even pewter, platters but many preferred still to eat from trenchers of brown bread, large rounds of bread cut from four-day old loaves with the centre hollowed out. After the meal these trenchers, soaked in meat or fish juices and sauces, were gathered up into baskets and given to the poor.

Breadcrumbs were used to thicken sauces and custards and slices of toasted bread were placed in the bottom of bowls of soups and stews to add body to them.

In the abbey barley was ground to bake bread and oatcakes were common fayre. Weed seeds usually found their way into the bread flour and even beans, peas and acorns were added to the mixture when the harvest was poor. We called this "Horse Bread", only fit to feed to horses. Branny brown breads were not as poor as that. Baked mostly with bran they provided good nutrition for our servants, although they caused great winds to blow up!

28. Manchet

It will be difficult for you to make bread that tastes the way we used to enjoy it. However, this is my favourite recipe using ingredients that you will be able to find. You will need plain unbleached bread flour, preferably from a healthfood or wholefood shop. Buy the yeast from there, too. Using unbleached flour this loaf may be slightly yellow. This is normal.

2 teaspoons of instant yeast
1¾ cups of water
1 teaspoon of salt
2 tablespoons of sugar
3 cups of unbleached bread flour
1 egg white

To prepare one loaf of good white bread start by making a leavener. Put one cup of flour into a bowl with one cup of lukewarm water and add 1 teaspoon of instant yeast. Leave it to stand for three hours. When it has proved, mix it with two cups of flour and add the remaining water, salt, sugar and yeast. Mix well and knead thoroughly into a stiff dough. Rest the dough for an hour then shape it into a round loaf. Let it rise until it doubles in volume then brush the surface with egg white. Bake the loaf in an oven pre-heated to 375°F for 45 minutes or until golden brown. Let it cool for at least an hour.

29. Household Bread

Those of us in the cloister were not supposed to eat fine white bread such as manchet. Our fare was supposed to be household bread, baked from barley, which was thought to be more sustaining for the long hours we spent studying, toiling in the fields and praying. We brewed our own ale in the abbey so we always had plenty of barley about the place and our cooks provided loaves very much like these ...

1lb 2oz of strong wholemeal flour (you will find it best at healthfood or wholefood shops)
8oz of barley flour (from the same shop)
1oz of rice flour (ditto)
½ tablespoon of salt
½oz of fresh yeast
¹/₃ cup of ale
2 cups of warm water
2 teaspoons of clear honey
Olive oil

Mix the dry ingredients in a large warmed bowl. Blend the yeast with a little of the ale until it has the consistency of a cream. Mix 1½ cups of the water with the honey and add the yeast to the mixture. Stir the mixture into the dry ingredients until you have a firm dough, adding further cold water as necessary. Knead the dough until it stretches, then roll it into a ball. Lift the dough out of the bowl, lightly oil the inside of the bowl with olive oil and return the dough to the bowl. Cover the bowl with a clean linen cloth and leave it in a warm place until the dough has almost doubled in size. Briefly knead it and then pull it into two equal portions, shaping each into a roughly rectangular loaves and put each one into a bread tin or deep cake tin (with a removable bottom). Decorate the centre of each loaf with a cross-cut. Cover the dough lightly with a linen cloth and leave it in a warm place until well risen. Pre-heat the oven to 450°F and bake the loaves for 20-25 minutes. Test them with a metal skewer, which should come out clean. If they need a few minutes longer cover them with greased foil to prevent the crust darkening and slightly reduce the heat. Cool the loaves on a wire rack under a linen cloth. Do not try to slice them until they have completely cooled.

30. Cruste Rolle

A favourite supper in the cloister was frumenty served with these tasty cakes.

¼ teaspoon of saffron strands (or a few drops of yellow food colouring)
2 tablespoons of boiling water
8oz of plain white flour
Salt
Butter
2 eggs
Lard (for frying)

Put the saffron or food colouring into the boiling water and leave until the water is a deep golden yellow and has cooled. Sift the flour and a pinch of salt together and rub in the butter until the mixture has the consistency of fine bread crumbs. Beat the eggs in the saffron water and mix them into the flour to make a firm dough. Do not let the dough become over-dry, adding extra cold water if necessary. Roll out the dough into a thin sheet and cut out six inch rounds. Lightly grease a heavy-bottomed frying pan with the lard and add the rounds of dough, one at a time, frying them on a moderately hot surface, turning once, until they are brown on both sides.

31. Paest Royall

You will find a number of recipes for pies in this little book and you may use any pastry dough that you favour (or that you can defrost from the supermarket freezer). However, if you would like to use an authentic pastry here is the recipe for "Royal Pastry".

4 cups of plain white flour
1 teaspoon of salt (optional)
1½ cups of butter
4 egg yolks, lightly beaten
2-4 tablespoons of ice cold water

Using a large bowl (preferably earthenware) mix the flour and salt. Cut in the butter with a blunt knife until the mixture is crumbly and the texture of coarse sand. Add the egg yolks. Knead the pastry. If it is too dry add the water, a tablespoon at a time as needed, until the pastry forms a ball and no longer sticks to the sides of the bowl. Separate the dough into two equal portions. Cover it with a towel (a linen tea towel is best) and let the dough rest for 10-15 minutes. Roll out one portion for the pie shell and the other for the pie lid.

V. Flans & Tarts

Our flaunes and crustards were the forerunners of your flans and custards. They could be savoury or sweet; meat, fish, vegetables or fruit set with egg yolks and cream and baked in pastry cases. Flans were part of our feast day menu and we thought them a great treat.

32. Tart de Bry

This delicious cheese flan could use any rich soft cheese. Brie was well known to us but it was costly, so we made do with local soft cheeses.

Pastry for one open tart or 24 very small tarts
6 egg yolks or 3 whole eggs
5oz of soft cheese without the rind cut off
¼ teaspoon of each of ground ginger and salt
Pinch of powdered saffron (or a drop of yellow food colouring)
¼ cup of sugar, to be used if you want to serve this flan as a dessert

Mix the cheese, eggs and seasonings by hand, mashing the cheese first, beating the eggs separately and adding them to the cheese (or use your blender). Continue beating or blending until the mixture is smooth and light. Half fill the shell or shells and bake them in an oven at 375°F for 15 to 20 minutes, until lightly browned. Do not over-cook. The filling in the tarts should have risen. They will subside when you take the tarts out of the oven but they should be slightly rounded when you serve them.

33. Flampoyntes

This recipe calls for a piece of fatty pork, which would have kept the pie filling moist. Your local butcher will not sell you such a cut (nor will Tesco) but will supply a leaner meat. To compensate, use a stock to moisten the pie filling. The filling should seem a little on the runny side before baking. This can be achieved very pleasantly by adding a goodly measure of wine to the stock! The cheese may be any that you like and any local farm cheese would probably serve better than a mass-produced Cheshire or Caerphilly. The spices in the original recipe are referred to as "gode powdours" which leaves the choice to the cook. You might use either Poudre Douce or Poudre Forte (my recommendation – see Appendix II). Serves 6 to 8.

1½lb of roast pork, bone and fat removed, boiled and diced small (reserve the stock to moisten the filling with an addition of wine)
1½ cups of grated cheese
Sugar to taste (no more than ¼ cup)
1½ tablespoons of ginger
1 teaspoon of cinnamon

1 teaspoon of cloves
Short crust pastry to cover a 9 inch pie shell with extra pastry to form the "arrow heads"
2 tablespoons of oil for frying

Bake the pie shell and set it aside. The meat should be diced or grated to the same size as the cheese. Mix the meat with the cheese, sugar and spices. Taste and adjust the seasoning. Add enough of the reserved stock (and wine) to moisten the mixture and then add it to the pre-baked pie shell. Roll out the extra pastry quite thinly and then cut out triangles about 1½ inches along each side. Fry the triangles in a little hot oil until lightly browned on both sides. Drain well and decorate the pie with the triangles by wedging their bases into the filling with the points upwards. Bake at 375°F for around 45 minutes or until the filling has set. Serve hot.

34. Tarte in Ymbre Day

The main ingredient of our recipe clearly is any well-aged cheese, although an alternative version used breadcrumbs, so I have included both for this Ember Day tart. Try it with either, or both if you prefer. A fine mature Cheddar is excellent for this recipe (although it was not available in my day!). Alternatively use any mature hard farmhouse cheese.

3-4 small onions, chopped
2 bunches of parsley, chopped
½ teaspoon each of sage, basil and thyme (and any others you favour)
1 cup of grated cheese (OR ½ cup of unseasoned bread crumbs)
8 eggs, beaten
1 tablespoon of melted butter
⅛ teaspoon of saffron or a few drops of yellow food dye
½ teaspoon of salt
¼ cup of currants
¼ teaspoon of sugar
⅛ teaspoon each of cloves and mace
One nine-inch pie shell

Sauté the onions and parsley and drain well. Mix the onions and parsley with all of the other ingredients and put them in the pie shell. Bake it at 350°F for 35-40 minutes or until the pastry is brown and the filling has set.

35. Lombard Custard

Lombard custard was a rich confection of eggs, cream, dates and prunes. During Lent, when rich dairy dishes were forbidden, almond milk or cream was used in place of dairy products.

Flans and Wine

8oz of plain flour
5oz of unsalted butter
½oz of icing sugar
1 egg yolk
3 tablespoons of cold water

1 level teaspoon of cornflour
1oz of caster sugar
3 large egg yolks
1 pint of double cream
A large pinch of saffron (or a few drops of yellow food colouring)
2oz of stoned dates, finely chopped
2oz of no-soak prunes, finely chopped

Make the pastry case by rubbing the butter into the flour and sieving in the icing sugar. Stir together, then beat the egg yolk with most of the cold water and add it to the mixture. Work the mixture quickly into a firm dough with a fork, adding the remaining water as necessary. Knead lightly until the pastry is smooth. Roll the dough out on a lightly floured board. Line a greased deep 8 inch flan ring or cake tin with a loose bottom. Crimp the edges and prick the base. Leave the case to rest in a cool place for half an hour. Line the pastry case with foil or greaseproof paper, put it on a pre-heated baking sheet and bake it at 400°F for 25 minutes. Remove the foil or paper for the last five minutes.

While the case is baking prepare the filling. Mix the cornflour and sugar in a bowl, add the egg yolks one at a time, beating until the sugar has dissolved. Heat the cream with the saffron or yellow colouring until just at the point of boiling, stirring to distribute the colour through the cream. Allow to cool for 5 minutes then strain it onto the egg mixture and whisk them together. Add more sugar if you think that the mixture needs it. Sprinkle the chopped fruit onto the pastry base and pour the custard over it. Return it to the oven and bake at 350°F for 30 minutes or until just firm but a little wobbly in the centre. Remove it from the oven and leave it to cool. You can serve it cold or slightly warm.

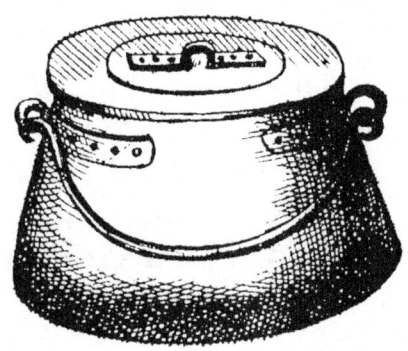

VI. Cheese, Dairy & Eggs

The abbey had many outlying estates with farms or "granges". These were kept for profit, leased to tenants or run by the abbey's own brothers (as was the great sheep flock at the place you call "Stow-on-the-Wold"). However, we also had our own farm, the "Barton", adjacent to the sacred precinct. We derived much of our own food from the Barton. Our dairy produced a variety of cheese. Hard cheeses were made from skimmed milk; soft cheeses were a sort of cream cheese made from whole milk and aged only briefly. "Grene" cheese was a fresh curd cheese drained on a bed of nettles or straw. Sometimes we added herbs and the cheese would be called "spermyse". The cheese used for many of our recipes was hard cheese. We did not have your delicious Cheddar cheese – that was first produced centuries after my day – and nor could we enjoy Stilton or just about any of your great cheeses. For the recipes in this book authenticity would best be served by going along to your favourite farm shop and buying a little of their best local cheese. Or you might say "hang authenticity" and use Cheddar! For soft cheeses use Brie (which is authentic) or any of your new British soft cheeses. We called cheese, and other dairy products, "white meats". Eggs were always useful. We stuffed eggs, we stewed eggs and we roasted them on spits as well as the usual poached, boiled, fried and scrambled. Butter was usually made salted for preservation and it was often necessary to remove the salt before using the butter in cookery (by clarifying it over a low heat) but you can simply buy unsalted butter.

36. Papyns

Do you enjoy a dish called "Eggs Benedict" (or should that be "Benedictine")? Then this dish of eggs served in a milky yellow sauce will meet with your favour.

1 cup of milk
¾ cup of flour
Several pinches of saffron (or a couple of drops of yellow food colouring)
¼ cup of honey
3 eggs

Put the flour and milk into a saucepan and blend it into a smooth sauce. If it seems too thin add flour and add milk if too thick. Add the honey and saffron, put the pan on the heat and bring to a low boil, stirring all the time to prevent it sticking. Do not let it boil vigorously. The sauce must be a golden yellow so add saffron as necessary until you have a pleasing shade. Reduce the heat. Put one or two inches of water into a deep frying pan (depending on how deep your pan is) and bring it to a simmer. Add a spoonful of vinegar to the water. Break each egg carefully into a cup or saucer, taking care not to break the yolk, then carefully slide the egg into the water to poach. Leave the eggs to poach only as long as it takes to cook the yolks; do not over-cook them. Remove the eggs from the water with a perforated spoon and place them on a serving dish. Pour the sauce over the eggs and season with salt and pepper to taste.

37. Arbolettys

This is a version of your scrambled eggs, flavoured with cheese and herbs. You can use your popular Cheddar cheese but it would be more authentic to use any locally made farm cheese of a similar texture.

2 tablespoons of milk
1 tablespoon of butter
1oz cheese (Cheddar or similar)
2 eggs
1 leaf of fresh sage, chopped
¼ teaspoon of powdered ginger
¼ teaspoon of powdered galingale
1 sprig of fresh parsley, chopped

Put the milk, butter and cheese into a frying pan and bring it to the boil. Break the eggs into a bowl and scramble them lightly with a fork. Add the herbs and spices to the eggs. When the cheese has melted add the egg mixture to the frying pan and stir it in. Cook it until it is as firm as you like then turn it out onto a plate and serve it hot.

38. Longe Fretoure

This is a quick and tasty recipe for one, with the unusual combination of cheese for flavour and sugar to sweeten. You can make the recipe by omitting the ale and using one whole egg instead of two yolks.

2 tablespoons of cottage cheese
2 egg yolks, beaten
2 tablespoons of ale
2 tablespoons of plain flour
½ teaspoon of sugar
1 tablespoon of lard

Put the egg yolks (or the whole egg) into a basin with the ale and cheese and beat them together. Then add the flour and beat the mixture until the batter is smooth. Heat the lard in a frying pan and add the batter. Cook it until it is firm, turning once. Cut the fritter into small squares using a spatula and cook them until they are light brown. Turn the pieces out onto a plate, sprinkle them with sugar and serve them hot.

39. Bruet of Egges to Potage

This is an unusual soup combining the flavours of cheese, eggs and lemon.

4 cups of water
6 tablespoons of butter
8oz of mild cheese, grated
4 eggs, well beaten
2 tablespoons of lemon juice
Salt
Pepper

Bring the water to the boil in a saucepan, add the butter and cheese and simmer the mixture, stirring it until the cheese has melted. Remove the mixture from the heat and stir in the eggs and lemon juice. Return the pan to a very low heat until it is smooth and has reached the thickness you prefer. Do not let it boil. Taste, season and serve.

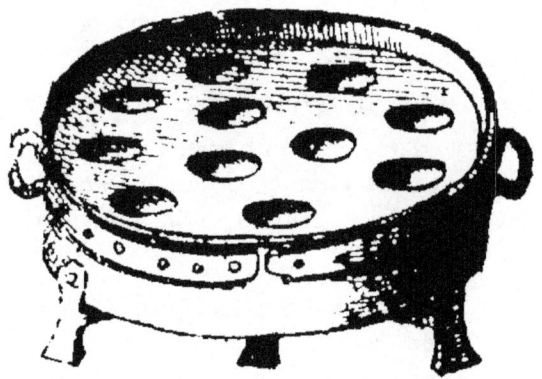

VII. Desserts & Sweets

Although the food allowed under the original rule of the Benedictine order was austere (our early monks were big on gruel, and bread and cheese) by the fifteenth century the restrictions had mellowed with custom and usage and we were able to enjoy sweet dishes, spiced toasts, pastries and delicious titbits. Candied fruits were common because our hives produced enough honey for us to use some in preserving. Even though the restrictions may have eased there were brothers who found ways round those few that remained and complaints about riotous and gluttonous monks were not uncommon. Which puts you in a rather stronger moral position than we were as you try these recipes ...

40. Shrewsbury Cakes

These are small delicate cakes flavoured with rosewater and nutmeg. Delicious treats!

½ cup of butter, softened
½ cup of sugar
2 tablespoons of rosewater
2½ cups of flour
½ teaspoon of nutmeg
½ teaspoon of salt

Cream the butter and sugar. Add the rosewater and blend thoroughly. Sift together the 2 cups of flour, nutmeg, and salt and stir into the butter until the dough holds together. With your hands, gently knead in enough of the additional flour to make a smooth ball of soft dough. Roll out on a floured board to the thickness of ½ inch. Cut large rounds with a glass or pastry cutter. Place the rounds on a greased sheet or one lined with parchment paper and bake in a 300°F oven for about 15 minutes, or just until done; they must be white, not brown. Remove the cakes to a rack to cool. You should have enough dough to make 20-25 cakes.

41. Apple Fritters

We enjoyed fritters, both sweet and savoury, and apple fritters were often on our menu owing to the abundance of apple trees in the Vale of Evesham. For the same reason we often enjoyed pear fritters. You can substitute firm pears for apples in this recipe.

6 eggs
2 cups of flour (approximately, using more or less as needed)
1 packet of yeast (used as a starter in brewing)
¼ cup of warm, stale ale (that is ale that has been allowed to allowed to go flat)
Pinch of saffron (or a drop of yellow food colouring)

Flans and Wine

½ teaspoon of salt
¼ teaspoon of pepper
4-6 large apples, peeled or unpeeled and sliced
Olive oil for frying
Sugar

Beat the eggs and flour into a slightly thick batter. Dissolve the yeast in a little warm ale and blend to a paste then beat it into the batter. Colour with the saffron or food colouring and add a little salt and pepper. Set the mixture aside while you cut the apples into medium-sized slices. Discard the seeds and stems. Coat the slices with the batter and fry them in hot olive oil until golden brown. Remove the slices from the oil and drain them well, sprinkle with sugar and serve.

42. Bryndons

The pleasing visual effect of this dish is of a yellow confection with a red topping, softened and flavoured with a spiced wine syrup. If you have saffron and sandalwood (as a herb, not as a soap!) then use these but yellow and red food colouring serve very well. Currants are what we called "Raisins of Corinth" and we sometimes used shredded almonds instead of pine nuts.

4½ cups of flour
2 cups of sugar
½ cup of cold water
Saffron (or a few drops of yellow food colouring)
Sandalwood (or a few drops of red food colouring)
¼ teaspoon of salt
Vegetable oil
1 bottle of inexpensive sweet red wine
1½ cups of honey
½ cup of red wine vinegar
1 teaspoon of white pepper
1 teaspoon of cloves
1 teaspoon of mace
½ cup of chopped dates
½ cup of currants
½ cup of pine nuts
1 cup of diced figs

Put a little of the wine into a saucepan and simmer the figs, then set them aside. Put the honey and the rest of the wine into a saucepan and bring the mixture to the boil. Skim off the scum as it arises until the mixture is clear. Add the vinegar, sandalwood or red colouring, white pepper, cloves, mace, dates, currants and pine nuts and return to the boil, then reduce the heat to a low simmer. In a separate bowl mix the flour, sugar and salt. Stain the water with the saffron or yellow colouring then slowly work enough of the water into the flour to

Flans and Wine

make a smooth paste, not over-wetting it, until it is the consistency of pie crust pastry. Roll the paste out on a floured board and cut into strips one inch wide by four inches long. Add oil to a deep frying pan, heat and quickly fry the strips of pastry until they are light brown and very crisp. Drain the strips then arrange them on a serving dish. Spoon the fruit and nuts on to the strips and soak them in the syrup.

43. Payne Foundow

Payne Foundow, a sort of bread pudding, was a sweet dish that we enjoyed with Caudell (***recipe 70***). The flavour is spicy and fiery, flavoured with preserved ginger. We did not have very much fresh ginger: it was not common in England until the sixteenth century. If you look for preserved ginger in your supermarket you will probably find it in the "Ethnic Food" or "Oriental" section. It is sweet and sticky as well as fiery and adds a flavour and texture to Payne Foundow that you will miss if you use fresh ginger root. Preserved anise seed might be difficult to find. You may have to look in a specialist food shop or an Asian supermarket.

1 loaf of slightly stale white bread
½ cup of butter (more authentic) or cooking oil (more modern)
Whites of 3 eggs, lightly beaten
1 cup of honey
¼ cup of water
2 cups red wine (Bordeaux is good)
1 cup of raisins
½ teaspoon of mace
½ teaspoon of pepper, cubeb, garlingale, cinnamon and nutmeg
¼ teaspoon of cloves
¼ teaspoon of salt
½ cup minced preserved ginger
Preserved anise seed

Cut the bread into small pieces and fry in the butter or oil until golden brown. Drain the bread. In a separate pan put the honey, egg whites and water and bring just to the boiling point. Skim off the scum. When completely clean remove the pan from the heat. Add the honey mixture to the bread then add all of the other ingredients except the anise seeds. Blend the mixture well. You can do this by hand or you can use a blender. If you use a blender hold back the ginger and add it after blending or it will clog your blades. The mixture should be stiff enough to stand on its own. If it seems too thick add a little wine; if too thin add more bread.

Payne Foundow was often served cold with a sprinkling of anise seed. However, you might prefer to place the entire mixture in a greased baking dish and bake it at 400°F for around 20 minutes, until it has set and has started to brown on top.

44. Tourteletes in Frytour

Figs were eaten as a treat all through Lent, particularly during the week before Easter, when we ate them to remember Christ's progress into Jerusalem.

1lb dried figs
Poudre forte
¼ teaspoon of saffron strands (or a few drops of yellow food colouring)
¼ teaspoon of salt
1 egg, separated and 1 egg white
6-7 sheets of filo or strudel pastry
Olive oil
1 cup of clear honey

Soak the figs in water, drain and either mince them or chop them very small. Save the liquid from the soaking, using a few drops to moisten the saffron, if you use it. Put the minced figs, spices, saffron (or food colouring) salt and egg yolk into a bowl and mix them well (you may use your food mixer). Lay a sheet of pastry flat, beat the egg whites until they are liquid and then brush the top side of the pastry with the beaten egg white. Cut the pastry into 3 inch wide strips (cutting across the short edges). Put a dab of fig mixture on the end of each strip and roll it up, pinching the ends to seal the mixture in. Go on until you have used up all of the pastry and the fig mixture. You can either deep fry or shallow fry the rolls, to taste and serve them hot or cold. If you like a hot sweet treat, warm the honey until it is liquid and spoon it over the rolls.

45. Frumenty

Frumenty was one the most popular and versatile foodstuffs of the Middle Ages, used as an accompaniment to roast meat (venison being particularly favoured). However, this particular recipe was intended for Lent and was meant to be served with boiled porpoise, one of the restricted range of meats that we were permitted in the Lenten period. Porpoise is not compulsory!

1 cup of cooked bulgur wheat (or barley)
3 cups of Almond Milk
1 pinch saffron (or a few drops of yellow food colouring)
½ teaspoon of salt

Stir together all the ingredients. Bring to a gentle boil, stirring occasionally to prevent sticking, then reduce heat to low, cover and cook for about 45 minutes, or until the mixture becomes thick. Be careful not to scorch it. Serve as a soup or as a sauce for meat.

46. Fritter for Lent

While we are on the topic of food for Lent consider this recipe for a sweet fritter, which comes out quite like one of your pancakes.

1 cup of Almond Milk
¾ cup of flour
2 tablespoons of olive oil
1 cup of sliced figs and currants

Mix the Almond Milk quickly with the flour to make a pancake-like batter. Do not over beat it. If the batter is too thick dilute it with a little Almond Milk; if too thin, thicken with a little more flour. Heat the oil in a frying pan. When hot and starting to smoke, pour in half of the batter. Sprinkle the fruit over top and then cover with the remaining batter and cook until brown underneath. Then flip it over to brown the opposite side. Serve whole or sliced dredged with honey or sugar, if you like. If you are making more than one fritter heat your oven to 250°F a keep them warm before serving.

47. Pokerounce

This tasty sweetmeat is very quick and easy to make. The black pepper and spices in the mixture reduce the sweetness so the dish is not too sickly despite being made mainly of honey. However, one word of warning: pokerounce uses three ingredients that were reputed to stimulate desire. Because it contained honey, ginger and pine nuts we considered it an aphrodisiac, so perhaps it is surprising that it was frequently served in the monastery. Or perhaps not ...

8oz of good honey (buy it from a farm shop if possible)
½ teaspoon each of ground ginger, cinnamon and black pepper
4 thick slices of bread cut from a white loaf
A double handful of pine nuts
½ teaspoon of freshly grated nutmeg is optional but I recommend that you try it.

Measure the honey into a small saucepan. Add the spices, put the mixture on the heat and bring it to a simmer. Simmer it over a low heat for a few minutes until it is well blended. Do not let the honey mixture get too hot or it will caramelise. A froth will form on top and you may skim this off, although we did not. Allow the mixture to cool while lightly toasting the four slices of bread on both sides. Cut each slice of bread into four pieces, either triangles or rectangles and arrange them on a plate. Spoon the spiced honey over the toasted bread, taking care not to burn yourself on the hot honey. Decorate the bread with patterns of pine nut kernels set upright in the glaze. Serve it hot and eat it with a knife and fork to avoid burning your fingers!

VIII. Soups & Pottages

I have chosen a selection of dishes that you would call soups and pottages (thick soups) although we did not make the same kind of distinction that you do. Thicker pottages crossed over with meat and fish stews; vegetables and fruit could be prepared and served in the same way. In fact, if you want to prepare vegetables to go with any of these recipes, you can take beans, parsnips, carrots and mushrooms and simply boil them in stock. If you are feeling more adventurous you can add leeks or onions to the mixture. Pottages can be sweet as well as savoury so you will find a sweet recipe below.

48. Potage Fene Boiles

"Fene" is an early spelling of a type of white bean, often used to refer to other types of bean. As with the recipe for fried beans (**recipe 65**) fava beans are probably your most authentic modern equivalent.

2 cups of cooked fava beans, mashed
3 cups of almond milk
2¼ cups of cheap sweet white wine
1 cup of raisins
½ cup of honey

Put two cups of wine into a saucepan with the raisins and bring to the boil. Remove the pan from the heat and allow it to steep until the raisins have absorbed enough of the wine to make them plump. Slowly heat ½ a cup of the milk. When warm, carefully whisk the mashed beans into it. Add the remaining ¼ cup of wine and the honey. Still slowly cooking the mixture, beat in more milk until the mixture has a thick, smooth consistency. Drain the plump raisins and stir them into the pudding. Cook the pudding for another minute or two until the raisins are warm, then serve.

49. Jowtes of Almaund Mylke

We ate this soup all year round, but especially in Lent. It should come out a rich dark green and is very filling. You may make a complete meal of it if you serve it with *cruste rolles* (**recipe 30**). To prepare the leeks you will need to strip the green ends to expose the tightly folded green part at the top of the white stem. You will use this green part. Keep the white parts for the *slyt soppes* (**recipe 67**).

2lb of spinach
4oz of inner green leeks (see above)
2 tablespoons of any mixture of fresh chopped herbs that you like (chives, thyme and hyssop are very acceptable)
5 cups of water

Flans and Wine

4oz of ground almonds
½ oz of cornflour
Salt
Pepper
Pinch each of sugar and grated nutmeg

Remove the stalks of the spinach and wash the leaves thoroughly. Slice the leeks thinly. Strip the leaves of the herbs from their stems and chop them. Put the spinach leaves, leek greens and chopped herb leaves into a large pan and add the 5 cups of water. Put it on the heat and bring it to the simmer. Cover the pan and continue gently to simmer until the slices of leek are tender. Meanwhile put the ground almonds and cornflour into a small saucepan and add enough water to let you mix the almonds and flour into a creamy paste. Drain the spinach and leeks and put the liquid aside. Chop the leaves and puree them (we used a spoon and a sieve but you might want to use your blender or food processor) stir in the almond paste and half of the reserved cooking liquid. Add the salt and pepper, sugar and nutmeg to taste. Return the mixture to the saucepan and simmer, stirring all the time, until it is heated through and slightly thickened. Add the extra liquid if the soup needs to be thinned and dole out into bowls or fill a tureen to serve.

50. French Pot Herbs

We used to cook "white" peas, different from your modern green varieties. You may be lucky enough to find medieval white peas otherwise you will have to make do with green peas, fresh or frozen.

2lb of peas, shelled (fresh or frozen)
Fresh herbs in any combination: parsley, thyme, mint, sage, basil and any others you fancy from Appendix I chopped small
1 cup of peeled pearl onions or the white heads of spring onions
2-3 tablespoons of olive oil
Salt
Pinch of saffron (or a drop of yellow food colouring)
Poudre Douce

Boil the peas until they are very tender, remove them from the water and drain them. Mash the drained peas by hand (or using your trusty blender). Put the mashed peas into a large saucepan on a very low heat. In a separate saucepan parboil the fresh herbs then remove them from the water and dry them. Lightly chop the herbs then stir them into the purée. Boil the onions until they are tender and add them to the purée along with the olive oil, saffron (or yellow food colouring) and salt to taste. Turn up the heat and allow the soup to bubble for several minutes, stirring it often to keep it from sticking. Turn the soup out into a serving dish and sprinkle with Poudre Douce (see Appendix II).

51. Cawdel of Muskels

Shellfish were one of our special treats during the Lenten season, the 40 days leading up to Easter, a period in which we fasted by avoiding meat – any animal that lived on land. Shellfish were safe. Sometimes our cook prepared them simply in a stock of their own juices fortified with ale; sometimes he cooked a rich pottage like this one.

3lb of fresh mussels
2 tablespoons of dry white wine
1 small white onion, chopped very small
8oz of leeks, sliced very thin
2 tablespoons of olive oil
1½oz of ground almonds
2 teaspoons of ground ginger
A large pinch of saffron (or a few drops of yellow food colouring)
¾ pint of fish stock
Salt and freshly milled black pepper
1 tablespoon of white wine vinegar
4 tablespoons of double cream

Wash and scrub the mussels very thoroughly, scraping off any barnacles, removing the beards and discarding any mussels that do not open when sharply tapped. Put the mussels in a large pan and add a splash of the wine. Cover the pan and cook on a high heat for 4-5 minutes, shaking the pan until the mussels have opened. Strain the liquid into a bowl and set it aside. Heat the oil in a saucepan and fry the leeks and onions for around 3 minutes until they have softened. Add the remaining wine and boil until the liquid has reduced by half. Stir in the ground almonds and spices. Mix the cooked liquid with the fish stock and gradually add it to the pan, stirring well all the time. Leave the pan to simmer for 25 minutes. Liquidise the contents of the pan and strain into a clean saucepan. Taste the liquid, season and sharpen with the wine vinegar. Discard one half of each mussel shell. Bring the liquid back to the boil, reduce the heat and stir in the cream and mussels. Serve immediately with fresh crusty bread.

52. Apple Muse

This is a fruit pottage (as I said, pottages did not have to be savoury) a thick, blended dish that could be made from dozens of different ingredients in a variety of different ways. Pottages were very popular both inside the cloister and outside it. As with other dishes Apple Muse can be made as thick as a pudding or as thin as a thick soup, and can also be served either hot or cold (although we thought that it was best eaten just after being cooked). Feel free to garnish with Poudre Douce (see Appendix II).

4-6 large apples, peeled cored and sliced
1-2 cups of Almond Milk
½ cup of honey

Flans and Wine

1-2 cups of unseasoned breadcrumbs
A few threads of saffron (or a few drops of yellow food colouring)
A few drops red food colouring
Salt to taste

Boil the apples until they are very soft; drain them and then mash them either by hand or using your trusty food processor until they are quite smooth. Place the apples in a large saucepan and blend in the Almond Milk, honey, breadcrumbs, spices and food colouring. Cook the mixture on a low heat, stirring every few minutes, until the pottage is completely hot and has thickened to the desired consistency (adding more bread crumbs as necessary). Serve immediately.

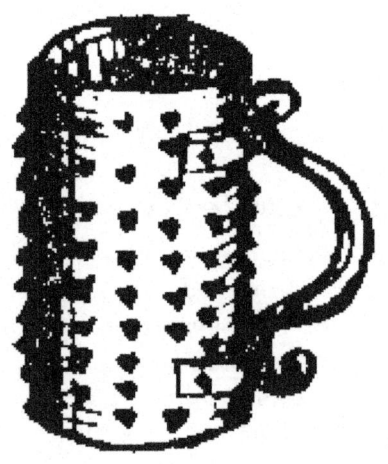

IX. Sauces

Sauces were essential to medieval cookery, flavouring foods that were otherwise prepared very simply. Meat and poultry were often just spit roasted, grilled or boiled in chunks. Fish were fried, grilled or poached. To fit these dishes to our taste they were served with an appropriate sauce, either poured on or provided separately for dipping. Sauces were usually highly spiced and often brightly coloured. I have also provided a recipe for that invaluable ingredient: Almond Milk.

53. Almond Milk

Fresh milk is something you are lucky enough to take for granted; in my day we did not have refrigerators and animal milk just would not keep. Our cooks rarely used it because they could not be sure that it would not have gone off by the time that they needed it. Sometimes we had milk that came straight from our own cows, either on the Barton (our farm attached to the abbey) or grazing at one of our granges but we never bought milk, for sellers of milk often sold either spoiled milk or watered good milk. Even fresh milk had to be used at once or turned into butter, cheese or cream.

Rather than animal milk our cooks relied on the milky liquid that resulted from grinding almonds or walnuts. This liquid is high in natural fats (it could even be churned into butter, like cow's milk) and Brother Kitchener had it prepared whenever it was needed in quantity. It could be prepared in anticipation without fear of it spoiling. And, a bonus for us, because it was *not* animal milk we could use it on our church's meatless days!

You can enjoy our recipes with cow's milk (full fat, not that watery skimmed substance you strange people seem to enjoy) but, if you want to try something different, and more authentic, then prepare a quantity of almond milk. Fortunately it is very easy to make.

Take one cup of ground almonds and two cups of boiling water. Mix the almonds into the water and leave them to steep for five minutes, stirring occasionally. We would have sieved the mixture to remove the coarse grains or might have used a mortar and pestle to blend the grains into the liquid. You, of course, can blend the mixture in an electric blender until the grains are completely absorbed. This will give you two cups of almond milk.

54. Cameline Sauce

Cameline sauce was ubiquitous in Western Europe and there were almost as many recipes as there were cooks. Almost the only thing nearly all they agreed on was that it contained cinnamon, and even that was not universal! This is a good basic recipe that was served with all sorts of meat. Add currants and nuts if you like a sweeter sauce for use with pork (for example).

Flans and Wine

1 cup of cider vinegar
1 cup of water
Fine unseasoned breadcrumbs
½ teaspoon of cinnamon
¼ teaspoon of ginger
¼ teaspoon of cloves
¼ teaspoon of mace
¼ teaspoon of grains of paradise or cardamom
Pepper and salt

Mix the liquids and spices thoroughly with a whisk. This sauce can be used without a binding agent or you can either thicken it by whisking or by blending in the breadcrumbs. Season to taste and either use immediately or refrigerate.

55. Galentyne

We used this sauce, served at room temperature, as an accompaniment to fish, fowl and roast meats. As made below it is a good "house-wife" sauce. On the other hand our cooks often used red wine vinegar and tempered it with 1 cup of dry red wine. This makes it a more mellow sauce, easier to take for refined tastes like yours.

1 cup of vinegar (red wine, cider or malt)
1 cup of unseasoned breadcrumbs
1½ teaspoons of galingale
1½ teaspoons of cinnamon
1½ teaspoons of ginger
Salt to taste

Mix the vinegar and spices then whisk in enough of the breadcrumbs to make a smooth slightly thickened sauce. Season to taste then strain or put through a blender to remove any lumps.

56. Saracen Sauce

This is another good accompaniment to meat and fowl, not unlike your Béchamel Sauce. We often coloured sauces with alkanet, a red dye derived from a plant root and Sarcenes dishes were often dyed deep red.

2 cups of almond milk
8 tablespoons of rice flour
A few threads of saffron (or a pinch of turmeric or a few drops of yellow food colouring)
½ teaspoon of ginger
½ teaspoon of mace
½ teaspoon of cubeb

½ teaspoon of cinnamon
1 tablespoon of sugar
½ cup of stock (without breadcrumbs) – see **recipe 57**.
Red food colouring
Salt to taste

Heat the almond milk slowly, blending in the flour until you have a very thick smooth sauce. Add the sugar and spices and blend in the stock. Use enough stock to thin the sauce to the consistency of gravy. Add enough food colouring to dye the sauce a deep red.

57. Stock

This is a tasty stock to be used in any dish. The recipe includes breadcrumbs to thicken and bind the sauce. You may add a little or a lot or you can make it without any breadcrumbs; thicken or not to your taste.

3 cups of chicken stock
1 cup of pork stock
½ to 1 cup of unseasoned breadcrumbs
½ teaspoon of pepper
½ teaspoon of cumin
Pinch of saffron or turmeric (or a drop of yellow food colouring)
Salt to taste

Mix the stocks and bring them to a simmer. Add the breadcrumbs (if required) and spices, bring back to the boil then reduce the heat and cook it for a further minute. Use it immediately or refrigerate it.

58. Strawberye

A spicy-sweet tangy sauce of strawberries that is a splendid accompaniment to plain roasted chicken. We would have blended with a sieve and spoon but you will probably want to use your blender. This recipe serves eight to ten.

1 cup of red wine
1 pound of fresh strawberries (you can use frozen at a pinch)
1 cup of strained almond milk
½ cup of currants
2 tablespoons of rice flour
½ cup of sugar
Pinch of white pepper
2 teaspoons of powdered ginger
1 teaspoon of cinnamon
½ teaspoon of galingale

Flans and Wine

4 tablespoons of red wine vinegar
1 tablespoon of butter
Pinch of saffron (or a drop of yellow food colouring)
Pomegranate seeds
Drop of red food colouring

Blend the strawberries, wine and almond milk until smooth. Pour the mixture into a saucepan and bring it to the boil. Add the rice flour as a thickening agent and stir until it thickens. Add the currants, red wine vinegar, butter and spices. Turn the heat down to medium and stir the mixture constantly for five minutes. Spoon the hot sauce into small bowls and garnish with pomegranate seeds.

59. Sauce Gauncile

A versatile sauce for a variety of foods. Goose, chicken and vegetables are greatly improved by adding this sauce, but do not limit yourself; try it with anything you favour.

1 cup of milk or almond milk
2 tablespoons of plain flour
2 cloves of garlic, peeled and crushed
Pinch of saffron (or a drop of yellow food colouring)
Dash of pepper
½ teaspoon of salt

Put the milk into a small saucepan and bring it to the boil. Reduce the heat, then add the flour and stir thoroughly. Add the garlic, pepper, saffron (or colouring) and the salt. Bring the sauce to the simmer and cook it for five to ten minutes, until it has thickened. Strain the sauce through a sieve into a serving dish or vessel and serve hot. You may wish to omit the saffron or colouring.

60. Poivre Jaunet

This is a very sharp sauce and may startle you if you are not expecting it. However, if you persevere you will come to enjoy its tart and unique taste. Adjust the spices to your personal taste – we did – because you may enjoy using less pepper and more ginger. The sauce can be as thin or thick as you like. It goes wonderfully with Pourcelet Farci (***recipe 11***).

2 cups of red wine vinegar
1 tablespoon of ginger
1 tablespoon of pepper
1 tablespoon of ground saffron (or 1 tablespoon of yellow food colouring)
½ teaspoon of cloves
1-2 cups of unseasoned toasted breadcrumbs (depends upon how thick you want the sauce)

Flans and Wine

Bring the vinegar to the boil in a saucepan. Reduce the heat slightly and beat in the spices and food colouring. Then slowly whisk in the breadcrumbs until you have the thickness you require. Continue beating until you have a smooth consistency and the mixture has again returned to the boil. Remove from the heat and serve hot as an accompaniment to roast meat.

61. Rapeye

This sauce was a favourite for pork dishes; it is a spicy, sweet and crunchy apple sauce. The recipe calls for almond milk but this is not the usual Almond Milk recipe (***recipe 53***). It uses white wine instead of water and the almonds are not crushed, but are left coarsely ground, and the milk is not strained. This recipe makes four helpings of sauce.

1 cup of white wine
¼ cup of dates (not the sugary kind you eat at Christmas) pitted and finely chopped
1 cup of unstrained almond milk
2 cooking apples, peeled, cored and chopped
½ teaspoon of powdered ginger
1 teaspoon of powdered cinnamon
½ teaspoon of powdered mace
¼ teaspoon of powdered cloves
½ teaspoon of powdered sandalwood
3 tablespoons of sugar
1 tablespoon of rice flour
Pinch of saffron (or a drop of yellow food colouring)

Put the apples, almond milk, wine, dates and spices into a large saucepan and bring it to the boil. Reduce the heat and simmer the mixture, uncovered, until the apples are very soft. Remove the pan from the heat and let the mixture cool. Then mash the apples and strain off the liquid. Put the mashed apples on one side. Return the liquid to the saucepan and bring it to the boil. Add the rice flour and stir the sauce until it thickens slightly. Strain the sauce and add it to the mashed apples. Stir well, pour into a serving dish and sprinkle with a dash of powdered cinnamon. Serve cold.

62. Compost

I have included this recipe at the risk of exciting unseemly mirth. The name refers to the combination (or "composition") of the ingredients and not to its use as a means of enriching your garden soil! Although the recipe is elaborate it is worth the effort to produce a splendid fruit and vegetable chutney.

1 bunch of fresh parsley, finely chopped
2lb of carrots, or parsnips or both, chopped into small pieces
2 small radishes, chopped into small pieces

Flans and Wine

2 large white turnips (not Swedish Turnips) chopped into small pieces
½ head of cabbage, shredded small
3-4 pears, peeled, cored and chopped small
1 teaspoon of salt
6 tablespoons of wine or cider vinegar
2 teaspoons of ginger
A few threads of saffron (or a few drops of yellow food colouring)
1 bottle of medium white wine
½ cup of honey
1 tablespoon of whole mustard seed
¾ cup of currants
1 teaspoon of cinnamon
1 tablespoon of Poudre Douce
½ tablespoon each of aniseed and fennel seed

Put the carrots, parsnips, turnips, radishes and cabbage into a large pan and boil them for several minutes until tender. Add the pears and the parsley and continue to cook until the pears have softened. Drain the pan. Put the vegetables and pears into a clean linen cloth and sprinkle them with salt. Allow it to cool then put everything into a large pan and add the vinegar, ginger and saffron or yellow food colouring. Cover the pan with the linen cloth and leave it to stand overnight. Next day put it in an air-tight non-metallic container (a kilner jar would be ideal). In a separate pan bring the wine to the boil then reduce the heat to a simmer. Add the honey and continue to simmer, skimming off any scum that forms. The mixture should be clear. Add the currants, cinnamon, aniseed and fennel seed. Continue to heat for several minutes then remove the pan from the heat and pour the contents over the vegetable mixture. Mix it well, leave it to cool and then seal the container. It may be stored for a week or ten days.

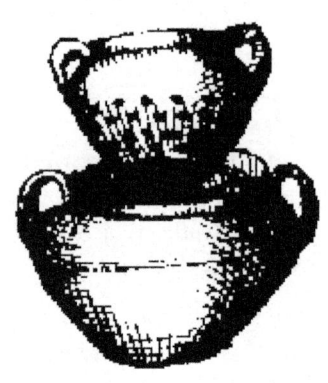

X. Fruit & Vegetables

Large walled gardens and orchards surrounded the buildings of our abbey, providing fruit and vegetables for our meals. The range of fruit and vegetables that was available to us was much more limited than in your day. At the same time we ate greens, salads, medicinal herbs, flowering plants, berries and unfamiliar parts of vegetables that are familiar to you. I will start with a local speciality ...

63. Dish of Asparagus

Those who know the Vale of Evesham will associate it with asparagus (or "gras" as we called it locally) so I thought that I had better include a recipe for preparing a dish of "gras", boiled asparagus, laid out on a platter with salt, oil and vinegar.. There were those among us who sprinkled it with herbs. Asparagus countered flatulence in the stomach, cleared the eyesight and softened the bowels. It was good for pains in the chest and spine and for all intestinal complaints. Sometimes we cooked it in wine and it was even more effective cooked this way. Remember that this was the fifteenth century!

A bundle of fresh asparagus, cleaned and trimmed (remove the woody lower part of each stalk)
Salt
Olive oil
Vinegar - red wine, white wine, or cider
Basil, thyme, savoury, hyssop, parsley or any other herb of the period (see Appendix I) in any combination that pleases you
Wine (optional)

Boil or steam the asparagus until it is just tender (do not overcook!). You can cook the asparagus either in water or in a mixture of two-thirds water and one-third wine. Place it in a serving dish, sprinkle a little salt and gently toss it with the vinegar and oil and then add a little of the chosen seasonings. Serve at once.

64. Spynoches Y-fryed

On occasion our cooks would insist on preparing a dish of vegetables so we used them to mop up the sauce of the main dish. One that we did enjoy was fried spinach, or other broad-leaved vegetables. If you use heavy vegetables whose leaves have a thick central rib you should remove the rib.

Broadleaf spinach or similar leafy vegetable
Olive oil
Salt

Pepper
Ground nutmeg
Ground cinnamon
Sugar

Clean the greens (and remove the ribs!). Fill a large saucepan with enough water to cover the leaves, bring it to the boil and blanch the leaves until they are just softened. Remove the leaves from the water and dry them. Heat the oil gently in a frying pan and add the spices, sugar and salt in equal quantities to taste. Stir them thoroughly into the oil then lay the leaves out in the frying pan, making sure that the leaves are coated with the oil. Turn the leaves after a minute then check after a further minute. If not yet tender then leave them in the oil for a little longer. Drain the leaves and serve them.

65. Fried Beans

Our medieval beans were primarily legumes not your modern green bean. The fava bean is probably the closest you will find to the sort of beans that we ate.

1lb of boiled fava beans
1 cup of finely chopped or minced onions
3-4 whole bulbs of garlic, separated into cloves
Olive oil
Powdre Douce to taste

Drain the boiled fava beans well. Combine them with the minced onion and the garlic cloves and sauté in hot oil until the onions & garlic are cooked and the beans have browned. Place into a serving dish and sprinkle on Poudre Douce to season. Serve it forth!

66. Salat

This is what you would call a lettuce and spinach "salad", a mixture of salad leaves with herbs and flowers. One herb that was used is rue. Warning: rue can induce labour in pregnant woman. This was not a problem in a wholly male community but you may wish to avoid this particular herb! Primroses and violets can be mixed in with the salad, or used as a garnish on top. Please use only fresh herbs. I have not given any quantities because you can use as much as you want and leave out any of the ingredients that you do not favour.

Parsley
Sage
Green garlic
Scallions
Lettuce
Leeks

Spinach
Borage
Mint
Primroses
Violets
Green onions
Fennel
Garden cress
Rue
Rosemary
Purslane
Olive oil
Wine vinegar
Salt

Rinse and wash the ingredients, remove stems etc., tear them up with your hands and toss them well with oil, vinegar and salt and "mess it forth". Use any variation of these ingredients to come up with your own personal "salat".

67. Slyt Soppes

This version of "sops in wine" was popular during Lent when we were (officially) supposed to eat only bread sops and water for supper. Although austere by our standards this dish would have been beyond the reach of the poor; it includes white wine in place of meat stock and uses luxurious ingredients such as olive oil and good white bread.

8 large or 12 medium leeks
2 tablespoons of olive oil
Salt
1 bottle of white wine
3-4 slices of soft white bread, freshly toasted

Remove the green parts of the leeks (the poor would have eaten the entire leek) and thinly slice the white parts. Put the sliced leeks into a saucepan with the wine, salt and oil and simmer them until the slices of leek are soft. Meanwhile break the toast into small pieces and divide them between six soup bowls. Spoon the leeks and hot wine into the bowls and serve as soon as the toast has softened.

XI. Drinks

Many of our alcoholic drinks were very sweet, flavoured with honey or with sugar. We had a "sweet tooth" as you might put it. If you find sweet drinks do not suit your modern palate then please feel free to reduce the amount of honey or sugar and taste only small quantities.

68. Clarrey

A good Clarrey, aged for a year or more, was a real delight to us. Clarrey was mulled wine flavoured with honey and spices. Its name came from our Latin "vinum claratum", that is "clarified wine". Today the same term survives for the red wine you call "claret", but in my day we used a sweet white wine for Clarrey.

1 bottle of sweet white wine (an inexpensive bottle will be nearer to our wines than an expensive vintage, whose flavour will be lost in the recipe)
1-2 cups of clear runny honey
1 tablespoon of cinnamon
1 tablespoon of galingale (or ginger)
1 tablespoon of cardamom
1 teaspoon of white pepper
You will need some cheesecloth to strain the wine

Prepare your clarrey at least one month before you plan to drink it. Put the wine and one cup of honey into a saucepan and bring slowly to the boil, then reduce the heat. A scum will form; skim it off. Taste the wine and add more honey if necessary. Remove the pan from the heat, stir in the spices, cover and leave the spiced sweetened wine to sit for 24 hours. During that time the spices will settle into a thick sediment in the bottom of the pan. Stretch two or three layers of cheesecloth across the mouth of another vessel and ladle the wine out of the pan, taking care not to disturb the sediment. Pour the wine slowly through the cheesecloth to filter out the last traces of the spices. Then bottle and cork.

A similar drink, but with even more spices, was Ypocras.

69. Potus Ypocras

Also called "Hipocras" this was a very popular drink at the abbey. It was named after the famous physician of ancient days called Hippocrates, because we believed that it had medicinal properties. We had several recipes for preparing Ypocras drink. This is one of the most common and you can use red wine or white as you please. This is another drink that improves with age. Keep it for at least one month before drinking. Keep it for a year if you can.

1 bottle of cheap sweet red or white wine (please do not use expensive wine)
1 to 1½ cups of sugar or 1 to 2 cups of honey, or a mixture
1 tablespoon of ginger
1 tablespoon of cinnamon
1 tablespoon of cardamom
1 tablespoon of white pepper
1 tablespoon of cloves
1 tablespoon of nutmeg
1 tablespoon of caraway seeds
You will need cheesecloth to strain the wine

Put the wine and 1 cup of sugar (or 1 cup of honey) in a saucepan and slowly heat until boiling. If you use honey a scum will rise as the mixture boils. Skim it off. Taste and sweeten further as necessary. Remove the pan from the heat, stir in all of the spices, cover it and leave it to sit from 24 hours, during which time the spices will settle as a thick residue. Stretch two or three layers of cheesecloth across the mouth of another vessel and ladle the mixture through to remove the remaining traces of the spices, taking care not to disturb the sediment. Bottle and cork.

70. Caudell

We drank caudell in small cups as a warming drink; we also used it as a sauce for sweet dishes. If you are tempted to use an expensive white wine, please do not. It will be wasted and would not be authentic. Our wine was cheap and sweet and we added sugar to make it more palatable.

Yolks of 5 eggs
²/₃ cup of white wine
Sugar to taste
Pinch of saffron (or a drop of yellow food colouring)

Beat the egg yolks, wine, sugar and saffron in a saucepan then heat the mixture over a medium flame, stirring continuously. The caudle will rise, thicken and become fluffy. It will also heat up so take care not to let it burn or stick to the pan. Serve at once.

Flans and Wine

APPENDIX I.   HERBS & SPICES

Many of the herbs we used were brought to this country by the Romans who established herb gardens when they settled in the countryside and built their rural villas. When the Romans withdrew from these islands we inhabitants of the monasteries took up the care and cultivation of the herbs. As we travelled between monasteries we shared seeds and information about how to grow and use them.

We grew our herbs in a small sheltered garden, as well as gathering them in the wild. There were strict rules about the care and harvesting of herbs and gathering was often accompanied by special prayers. We used the herbs for medicines, and for other purposes such as extracting dyes, as well as for cooking. However, the herbs listed below were used for flavouring our meat and they helped to relieve the effects on indigestion, as well!

Aniseed.   Aniseed, sometimes called "anise" or less commonly "anis", is native to the eastern Mediterranean region and southwest Asia. We used it in soups and stews, baking and sweet breads. Anise seed smell and taste like liquorice and their oil was used in liqueurs.

Balm.   Sometimes called "cure-all", "sweet balm" or "lemon balm" we used balm in salads, infusions in drinks and as an ingredient in stuffings.

Basil.   This was a great favourite with our cooks who used it in soups and stews, sauces, salads and stuffings. We also called it "sweet basil" and "herb royal".

Bay.   The bay tree originally came from the lands to the east. Also called "nobel laurel" and "sweet bay" we used it in soups, stews and casseroles, stock, syrups, sweet and savoury sauces and in cooking fish.

Borage.   With a pleasant cool cucumber flavour borage, also known as "burrage" and "bugloss", was used in salads as well as to flavour drinks.

Caraway.   Caraway seeds were useful because they held their flavour for months stored in close earthenware jars. Our cook usually added them towards the end of cooking a dish as a long simmer could turn it bitter, spoiling a flavour similar to aniseed and fennel. It was used with pork, duck and goose to counter the fattiness of the meat.

Cardamom.   There are several sorts of cardamom cloves. Green cardamom was the most commonly used in cooking and there was also white cardamom, black cardamom and false cardamom. It was reputed to ease digestion and also had aphrodisiacal properties.

Chickweed.   You might be surprised that we ate chickweed (I think it is generally regarded as a pest in your day) but it has a pleasant nutty flavour. We used "starweed" in salads and, boiled like spinach, as one of the vegetables we used to soak up spare gravy. It grows in winter so was always available to us.

Chives.   An excellent herb for the kitchen, we used it with butter and cheese and in garnishes and soups. We also knew it as "cives", "civet", "sweth" and "rush leeks".

Cleavers. Also known as "everlasting friendship" and "goosegrass", cleavers was another herb that we boiled as a vegetable. It tastes bitter but not unpleasantly so.

Cloves. Cloves are the flower buds of the clove tree, dried in the sun. In addition to its use as a culinary spice it had medicinal properties as an antiseptic, to treat certain intestinal disorders and to ease child delivery (not such a great problem for us). To flavour dishes we found it best to grind the clove to a powder.

Coriander. Here is a very useful herb, which you might know as "cilantro", "chinese parsley" and even "dizzycorn". We used its leaves and seeds to flavour meat and to add spice to stews and salads. We also used to chew the seeds to stimulate the digestion and to counter flatulence and the gripes!

Dandelion. Another weed with surprising uses under a variety of names: "pis en lit" (or "pee in the bed" in English) "lion's teeth" and "fairy clock". We particularly liked the fresh leaves scattered on salads.

Elder. Do not be put off by the smell of the elder, its flowers and berries were often used in syrups, cakes, puddings, pies and sweet dishes. We also called it "black elder", "bore tree" and "pipe tree".

Fennel. "Fenkel" or "sweet fennel" was a useful herb. The chopped leaves were used with fish, the seeds flavoured bread and cakes and the bulbous base could be eaten raw, steamed, boiled or braised. The seeds and leaves were also beneficial for a poor digestion.

Galingayl. Though it resembles ginger in appearance (it is related to ginger) it tastes little like ginger. In its raw form, "galangal" has an earthy smell and a pine-like flavour with a faint hint of citrus. It is said to have the effect of an aphrodisiac and to act as a stimulant.

Hyssop. Hyssop has a very strong flavour and, when our meat was past its best, hyssop was the best herb to make it palatable.

Lavender. We used lavender medicinally for its aromatic oil and as a flavour for all sorts of sweet and savoury food.

Marjoram. In the kitchen we used marjoram for flavouring all sorts of food including soups, sauces, salads and stuffing.

Marshmallow. The roots of the marshmallow look like parsnips but have a sugary taste. The seeds are edible and taste a little like hazelnuts. The roots (and leaves) yielded a jelly-like sap that was used to make the sweet "marshmallows".

Mint. We used many varieties of mint and, like you, we used it in drinks and sweets, sauces and garnishes. We also had to be careful to stop it taking over the garden.

Mustard. Both seeds and plants were used to make sauces and the plants were mixed with other herbs in salads and in other mixtures of leafy herbs.

Nettle. Stinging nettle, also known as "devil's leaf", "devil's plaything" and "tanging nettle", is another of those weeds whose leaves were cooked and eaten like spinach.

Nutmeg and Mace. Most people know nutmeg, which is the seed of a tree from the Indies. Not so many know mace, which is the outer covering around the nutmeg within the fruit of the nutmeg tree although both had medicinal properties as an analgesic. In England we preferred mace while the French favoured nutmeg.

Pepper. *Black pepper* is a flowering vine cultivated for its fruit which is usually dried and used as a spice and seasoning. The same fruit is also used to produce white pepper, red/pink pepper, and green pepper. Dried ground pepper was one our most common spices, prized for both its flavour and its use as a medicine. *Long pepper* is a close relative of the black pepper plant, and has a similar, though generally hotter, taste. Today, long pepper is a rare ingredient in European kitchens, but it can still be found in Indian vegetable pickles, some North African spice mixtures and in Indonesian and Malaysian cooking. It is readily available at Indian grocery shops, where it is usually labelled "Pipalli".

Purslane. Is a plant with a pinkish fleshy stem and small, round leaves; the leaves were used as a potherb or in salads. Boorde informs us that "purslane dothe extynct the ardor of lassyvyousnes, and doth mytygate great heate in all the inwarde partes of man".

Rose. A beauty to behold, rose petals were used to flavour honey and an infusion of the hips was used in jellies.

Rosemary. "Romero" was widely used as a strewing herb in church ceremonials. It was also widely used in the kitchen for flavouring meat and to flavour wine and vinegar.

Rue. Rue can induce labour in pregnant woman. Not a problem for a wholly male community but you may wish to avoid using it because of the potential danger involved.

Thyme. As a kitchen herb thyme (or "tomillo") was a favourite as a digestive and was widely used in dishes of fruit, fish and grilled meat and in a variety of drinks.

Appendix II. Spice Mixtures

Cooks made up a variety of spice mixtures, kept in stoppered jars and ready for use. There was no universal recipe for these mixtures; each cook had his own combination of a fairly standard set of ingredients. Rather like those who, in your day, use curry powder, a ready-made mix of spices, instead of preparing the spices fresh every time they cook. Two of the most common were Poudre Douce and Poudre Forte. Poudre Douce was always a mild, sweet, mixture. Poudre Forte combined black pepper, ginger and a variety of other strong spices.

Many of the recipes in this little book include sugar so I have appended a note on the type of sugar that we used.

Poudre Douce

Poudre Douce ("Sweet Powder") could be used in everything from stews to pastry. There were thousands of recipes (each cook had his or her own favourite) so this one is only an example and you can vary it to taste.

2 rounded tablespoons of ground ginger
2 rounded tablespoons of ground cinnamon
2 rounded tablespoons of bay leaves ground to fine powder
1½ teaspoons of ground cloves

You could add a tablespoon of sugar, a whole nutmeg (grated) or both.

Poudre Forte

Poudre Forte ("Strong Powder") could also be used generally in spices and sauces.

¼ cup of freshly ground black pepper
¼ cup of ground long pepper (or extra black pepper)
¾ teaspoon of ground cloves
1 whole nutmeg, grated

For a sweeter spice you may add cinnamon and ginger, but never sugar.

Sugar

Sugar was expensive in the fifteenth century. We did not have your cane sugar from the Indies. Our sugar came from North Africa in close-packed "loaves", white on the outside but treacly inside. The wealthy enjoyed the white sugar cut or scraped from the outside of the loaf. This sugar was similar in consistency to your granulated sugar but with coarser crystals. For fine dishes such as flans and custards use caster sugar.

APPENDIX III. CONVERSION TABLES

BROTHER WILLIAM'S MEASURES
1 tablespoon = 2 dessertspoons
1 dessertspoon = 3 teaspoons = ½ fl.oz
1 cup = 20 tablespoons = 60 teaspoons = 10 fl.oz
1 pint = 2 cups = 20 fl. oz = ½ quart
1 quart = 4 cups = 2 pints = ¼ gallon

IMPERIAL	METRIC	US VARIATIONS
1 ounce	28 grammes	
1 pound	454 grammes	
1 teaspoon	5 millilitres	
1 tablespoon	15 millilitres	
1 inch	2.54 centimetres	
1 fluid ounce	29 millilitres	
1 pint	570 millilitres	473 millilitres (liquid)
1 ¾ pints	1 litre	
1 quart	1.136 litres	0.946 litres (liquid)
1 gallon	4.546 litres	3.785 litres

GAS MARK	CENTIGRADE (°C)	FAHRENHEIT (°F)
1	140	275
2	150	300
3	160	325
4	180	350
5	190	375
6	200	400
7	220	425
8	230	450

Flans and Wine

FURTHER READING

If the 70 recipes in this little book have whetted your appetite you might like to look at some of the medieval cookbooks that are available today either in manuscript or republished as books. Europe's first cookbook (a book of recipes that was copied and passed on) was: "The Forme of Curye", compiled by the cooks of the ill-fated Richard II around 1390. The "Forme of Curye" is available today as part of a 14th century recipe collection called: "Curye on Inglish" (which sounds like it should star Leslie Philips) which also contains three influential manuscripts from the same era: "Diuersa Cibaria", "Diuersa Servicia" and "Utilis Coquinario". These four main resources provide a wealth of material for the beginning of the fifteenth century.

Appearing shortly after the publication of "The Forme of Curye" (and probably based on it) was a collection known today as: "An Ordinance of Pottage". It is in print today, with redactions by Constance B. Hieatt.

The next best source after these would probably be Thomas Austin's: "Two 15th-Century Cookery-Books", originally published in 1888, but featuring English manuscripts from 1425 - 1450.

Terence Scully's: "The Art of Cookery in the Middle Ages" provides an excellent background to understanding the nature of cooking and food production in the high Middle Ages.

Flans and Wine

INDEX OF RECIPES

Recipe	Number
Almond Milk	53
Apple Fritters	41
Apple Muse	52
Arbolettys	37
Beef or Mutton Olives	6
Boiled Mutton	2
Bourbelier de Sanglier	7
Brawune Fryes	5
Stock	57
Bruet of Egges to Potage	39
Bruet Sarcenes	13
Bryndons	42
Cameline Meat Bruet	14
Cameline Sauce	54
Caudell	70
Cawdel of Muskels	51
Chicken in Orange Sauce	15
Clarrey	68
Compost	62
Cormarye	8
Cruste Rolle	30
Dauce Egre	21
Dish of Asparagus	63
Dressed Crab	24
Egurdouce	1
Endored Chicken	17
Flampoyntes	33
French Pot Herbs	50
Fried Beans	65
Fritter for Lent	46
Frose	9
Frumenty	45
Galentyne	55
Goose or Capon Farced	18
Hen in Wine-Stock	16

Household Bread	29
Jowtes of Almaund Mylke	49
Lombard Custard	35
Longe Fretoure	38
Manchet	28
Mortress	10
Mounchelet	3
Neat's Tongue	4
Oystres in Cevey	23
Paest Royall	31
Papyns	36
Payne Foundow	43
Pike in Galentyne	27
Poivre Jaunet	60
Pokerounce	47
Potage Fene Boiles	48
Potus Ypocras	69
Poudre Douce	A.II
Poudre Forte	A.II
Pourcelet Farci	11
Pykes Brasey	25
Rapeye	61
Roasted Mallard	20
Salat	66
Saracen Sauce	56
Sauce Gauncile	59
Schyconys with the Bruesse	19
Seeth of Fresh Salmon	26
Shrewsbury Cakes	40
Slyt Soppes	67
Spynoches Y-fryed	64
Stew of Salmon	22
Strawberye	58
Sugar	A.II
Tart de Bry	32
Tarte in Ymbre Day	34
Tourteletes in Frytour	44
Venyson Y-bake	12

Printed in Great Britain
by Amazon